The Encrypted Book of Passwords:

The Encrypted Book of Passwords:

Raef Meeuwisse

Writing your passwords down is usually fraught with risks. The encrypted book of passwords helps you to store your passwords more securely in a format that only you can fully understand and use.

This **Hardback Edition** has several additional features above the standard pocketbook edition, including:

- A hardback cover.
- A *removable dust jacket* (to hide the title details from view).
- Allows over 500 accounts and passwords to be stored.

Cyber Simplicity Ltd
2016

Raef Meeuwisse, Cyber Simplicity Ltd, Hythe, KENT, UK CT21 5HE.

First Printing:	2016
Edition:	Second Edition, Hardback
ISBN	978-1-911452-02-7
Edition Date:	22 May 2016
First published by:	Cyber Simplicity Ltd

www.cybersimplicity.com

Ordering Information:

Special discounts are available on quantity purchases by corporations, associations, educators, and others. For details, contact the publisher at the above listed address. Trade bookstores and wholesalers: Please contact Cyber Simplicity Ltd.

Tel/Fax:	+44(0)1227 540 540 or
Email	orders@cybersimplicity.com.

Also Available

Also available from this author in paperback & digital formats:

Cybersecurity for Beginners

This book provides an easy insight into the essentials of cybersecurity, even if you have a non-technical background.

The Cybersecurity to English Dictionary

This book is designed to be a useful companion for anyone who wants to keep up on cybersecurity terms or confound others with their understanding.

Finally, cybersecurity does not need to sound like a different language.

The Encrypted Book of Passwords: Pocketbook Edition

A smaller format version of this book in a pocketbook size, with space for over 200 account and password entries is available. There is also a paperback version available at the same size as this edition. Corporate promotional versions are also available from our website.

Visit www.cybersimplicity.com for a full list of the latest titles.

Contents

Introduction

Using computers, mobile phones, tablets and the ever expanding number of other connected devices are becoming increasingly risky activities.

Every day, people are having their online identities compromised, resulting in varying levels of cost and inconvenience.

Working in the field of cybersecurity; friends, family, colleagues and small businesses increasingly asked me how to keep themselves safer from being compromised.

One of the simplest ways to reduce the risk of being compromised is to use different usernames and passwords for different accounts. However, the very high number of online accounts we are all now maintaining is getting unmanageable unless we have a better method to securely keep a record of that information.

At a security conference I attended in early 2015, the question was asked 'Who here keeps a separate password for each online account they use?' There were over 300 people in the room, only one hand was raised: '325 and counting' he said.

The reality is we should all be using separate passwords.

The main purpose of this book is to provide an easy way to securely store a physical copy of your accounts and separate passwords, without the usual risk associated with writing these details down.

This hardback edition has the added benefit of a removable dust jacket. Removing the dust jacket changes the book appearance to an unmarked, standard, blue cloth cover with no markings on the cover or spine.

1: Why Use This Book?

With the growth in the number of electronic accounts we each maintain, one of the biggest challenges we all face is remembering all those details and keeping them secure.

What makes life even harder is that many electronic passwords require complex combinations of letters, numbers and special symbols.

This book provides a solution that is designed to help address these problems. Finally, you can have a secure, readable and accessible hardcopy record of all your different usernames and passwords.

Some people try and overcome this problem by re-using the same password across many different accounts. For security reasons, this is highly dangerous and inadvisable. This is because, if any cyber criminal steals your username and password information from one place, one of the first things they usually do is to try those same details in many other online services.

So, for example, if you have a payment services account (PayPal or similar) and you chose to use the same email username and password information for another completely different account, if the other account information gets stolen, the chances are reasonably high that the criminals will try that same username and password information in other high value targets such as PayPal, Amazon and Ebay.

It is therefore very important that all of your passwords on any electronic accounts of value are different from each other.

You should never write (or type in) your username and account details *in full* anywhere, except when logging in and out of the system or application they are designed for. Yet, with the growth in the number of electronic accounts we each maintain, many of us do need to keep a secure record of these.

Although there are many great online services that can help to keep your details secure, most people, including many security professionals prefer to keep their information impervious from online threats by holding it in a physical format.

If used in the correct way (read chapters 2 & 3), this book will allow you to securely store a physical copy of over 500 different usernames and passwords.

If you need more – just order another copy of the book!

2: How to Use This Book

Remember; writing down your full username and password details anywhere is always a really bad idea.

However you can write most of it down as long as you keep at least part of it as secret information that only you know.

This book works by using a tried and tested security principle known as multi-factor authentication. Put simply, this just means that you are going to create at least one secret key that you will not write down in this book and only you will know.

If your encrypted book full of usernames and passwords is stolen, then it will still be of no use to the thief because none of the passwords will work without the secret piece of information that only you know.

For example, in a simple form, you might chose to use a 4 digit PIN (personal identification number) as your secret key. This secret key would be part of your complete password but would not be written down in this book or anywhere else.

If someone were to steal the book, they could still not access your accounts because they could not use your password unless they could also guess your secret key (in this case a 4 digit PIN).

To make your passwords even more secure, each time you make an entry in the book, you can mark in the book if you put that secret key at the start, end, middle or other indicated point in the password.

For example, let us say that I chose a simple secret 4 digit key of **9287**. In my book I would write my account details down as follows:

Account:	Ebay
Username:	**example_account@tebop.com**
Password:	**fr1edchick3n**
Secret Key: ☐Start ☑**End** ☐Middle ☐Indicated Point ☐Split
Key Used: ☑1 ☐2 ☐3 ☐4 ☐5☐6 ☐7

This would tell me that I have used my secret key (in this case a 4 digit PIN) at the end of the password.

The Encrypted Book of Passwords

My password in the book is recorded as *fr1edchick3n* but in reality, the password would be *fr1edchick3n9287*.

If someone tried to access this (fictional) Ebay account, although the username would be correct, the password would not be usable unless the person knew my secret key.

You will also notice that each account entry in the book:

- allows you to have more than one secret key
- and to place it in a number of different positions.

You can find more information on increasing the level of your password secrecy in the next chapter.

How sophisticated you want to keep the secret component is up to you. This book will offer tips and suggestions on how to do that.

There is also a HOME SECURITY NOTES section at the very back of the book with some simple home security tips that everybody can and should apply to help improve your general online security.

3: Increasing Password Security

As many of you will already have noticed, the format for each entry in this book allows you to have up to 7 secret keys;

Key Used: ☐ 1 ☐ 2 ☐ 3 ☐ 4 ☐ 5 ☐ 6 ☐ 7

and to place the secret key in up to 5 different locations;

Secret Key: ☐Start ☐End ☐Middle ☐Indicated Point ☐Split

Before we look at how to use these values, it is worth understanding which of your accounts may require higher levels of security.

Cyber criminals generally target online accounts based on the amount of monetary value they can directly or indirectly achieve. For example, in 2015, it was widely accepted that the full username and password details for any online payment account was generally worth 10% of the online balance.

Tip 1: Higher Security for High Risk Accounts

Although it is a great thought to put very high levels of security on all of your online accounts, the reality is that some of your accounts will be very low or zero value (for example - perhaps a free, online news subscription service) and some may be extremely high value (for example - your online bank log-in details).

It is advisable to apply many of the techniques described in this chapter to any online accounts that you consider to present the highest personal risk to yourself. That may be because they can directly access money, or it can be that they contain information of high value or even high embarrassment factor. (Where did I put my Ashley Madison log-in credentials?)

Tip 2: Hiding Account Names

For high risk or personally sensitive accounts, you do not need to record the real account name in this book, as long as you know what it means.

You can store your bank account name as 'Ornithology Today' as long as you know what the username and password really access.

If you do have any accounts that could be personally embarrassing, consider hiding those under false account names in this book, so that only you will recognize them.

The types of accounts that people often choose to hide can include any that inherently reveal health or other personally sensitive information, such as political opinion, dating preferences or other sensitive affiliations.

Tip 3: Use a Complex Secret Key

In place of the simple 4 digit PIN we used in chapter 2, it is more advisable to choose your secret key with greater complexity. As an example *r@3R* is still only 4 characters long but has 4 different types of characters. Consider choosing a secret key for your most sensitive accounts that includes:

- a lower case letter
- a special character
- a number
- an upper case letter

Tip 4: Have More Than One Secret Key

For each entry, this book allows you to use up to 7 different secret keys:

Key Used: ☐ 1 ☐ 2 ☐ 3 ☐ 4 ☐ 5 ☐ 6 ☐ 7

As long as you can remember the secret information, I would advise creating at least 3 secret keys for low risk, medium risk and high risk accounts.

You can also use more than one key on the same password as long as you can remember what order you used them!

Tip 5: Vary Where You Place Your Secret Key

You do not always have to put your secret key at the end of the password, there are five different positions offered:

Secret Key: ☐Start ☐End ☐Middle ☐Indicated Point ☐Split

If you mark 'middle' – make sure your written password has an even number of characters, so you know where to insert your secret key.

If you mark 'Indicated Point', you will need to decide on what mark to place in your password (a large 'X' perhaps) to show where the secret key needs to be inserted.

It is up to you how to use 'Split'. However, I would take the first 2 characters of my secret key and place them at the front of the password and the last 2 characters and place them at the end.

Tip 6: Keep It Simple

The most effective security keeps the criminals out but still lets you have easy access.

You should ideally use secret keys that you can easily remember and do not need to write down. As long as you maintain at least 2 secret keys, do not write those keys down and vary the placement of those keys, you should have a reasonable (but not perfect) level of security.

Tip 7: Double Entry

A back-up copy is always worthwhile. Having a second copy of your encrypted password book will help if you lose the first copy, as long as you maintain identical entries in both and store them in different locations.

Tip 8: Store This Book Securely

If you use this book in line with the instructions, it is designed to help keep your accounts, usernames and passwords accessible yet secure through the use of one or more separate **secret keys that you must never write in this book.**

However, you should still aim to keep this book somewhere secure, such as a locked draw, or other location where you might keep other valuable items.

Tip 9: If a Copy of Your Book is Stolen

If a copy of your password book does get stolen, it is worthwhile to change your passwords and change your secret keys, especially for any higher value or higher risk accounts.

Remember: A stolen copy of this book together with the full password from a compromised account can expose your secret key.

Tip 10: Do Not Use a Guessable Key

If you use a simple and easy to guess 4 digit number such as *0000*, or *1234* or *9999*, then it will still be relatively easy, if anyone steals your book, to access your accounts.

Make sure you use as complex a secret key as possible – see *Tip 3*.

Remember the 3 Golden Rules:

1. Always keep at least part of your password secret using a key that only you know.

2. Never write your secret key/s out, (if you do, never store them inside or near this book.)

3. Never re-use an identical password on any online account of value.

If you have not yet read the chapter on '**How to Use This Book**' (Chapter 2), please go back and read that section before entering information into this section.

A

Account: _____	Additional Notes:
Username: _____	_____
Password: _____	_____
Secret Key: ☐Start ☐End ☐Middle ☐Indicated Point ☐Split Key Used: ☐ 1 ☐ 2 ☐ 3 ☐ 4 ☐ 5 ☐ 6 ☐ 7	_____

Account: _____	Additional Notes:
Username: _____	_____
Password: _____	_____
Secret Key: ☐Start ☐End ☐Middle ☐Indicated Point ☐Split Key Used: ☐ 1 ☐ 2 ☐ 3 ☐ 4 ☐ 5 ☐ 6 ☐ 7	_____

Account: _____	Additional Notes:
Username: _____	_____
Password: _____	_____
Secret Key: ☐Start ☐End ☐Middle ☐Indicated Point ☐Split Key Used: ☐ 1 ☐ 2 ☐ 3 ☐ 4 ☐ 5 ☐ 6 ☐ 7	_____

Account: _____	Additional Notes:
Username: _____	_____
Password: _____	_____
Secret Key: ☐Start ☐End ☐Middle ☐Indicated Point ☐Split Key Used: ☐ 1 ☐ 2 ☐ 3 ☐ 4 ☐ 5 ☐ 6 ☐ 7	_____

Account: _____	Additional Notes:
Username: _____	_____
Password: _____	_____
Secret Key: ☐Start ☐End ☐Middle ☐Indicated Point ☐Split Key Used: ☐ 1 ☐ 2 ☐ 3 ☐ 4 ☐ 5 ☐ 6 ☐ 7	_____

Account: _____   Additional Notes:

Username: _____   _____

Password: _____   _____

Secret Key: ☐Start ☐End ☐Middle ☐Indicated Point ☐Split
Key Used: ☐ 1 ☐ 2 ☐ 3 ☐ 4 ☐ 5 ☐ 6 ☐ 7   _____

Account: _____   Additional Notes:

Username: _____   _____

Password: _____   _____

Secret Key: ☐Start ☐End ☐Middle ☐Indicated Point ☐Split
Key Used: ☐ 1 ☐ 2 ☐ 3 ☐ 4 ☐ 5 ☐ 6 ☐ 7   _____

Account: _____   Additional Notes:

Username: _____   _____

Password: _____   _____

Secret Key: ☐Start ☐End ☐Middle ☐Indicated Point ☐Split
Key Used: ☐ 1 ☐ 2 ☐ 3 ☐ 4 ☐ 5 ☐ 6 ☐ 7   _____

Account: _____   Additional Notes:

Username: _____   _____

Password: _____   _____

Secret Key: ☐Start ☐End ☐Middle ☐Indicated Point ☐Split
Key Used: ☐ 1 ☐ 2 ☐ 3 ☐ 4 ☐ 5 ☐ 6 ☐ 7   _____

Account: _____   Additional Notes:

Username: _____   _____

Password: _____   _____

Secret Key: ☐Start ☐End ☐Middle ☐Indicated Point ☐Split
Key Used: ☐ 1 ☐ 2 ☐ 3 ☐ 4 ☐ 5 ☐ 6 ☐ 7   _____

Account: _____	Additional Notes:
Username: _____	_____
Password: _____	_____
Secret Key: ☐Start ☐End ☐Middle ☐Indicated Point ☐Split Key Used: ☐ 1 ☐ 2 ☐ 3 ☐ 4 ☐ 5 ☐ 6 ☐ 7	_____

Account: _____	Additional Notes:
Username: _____	_____
Password: _____	_____
Secret Key: ☐Start ☐End ☐Middle ☐Indicated Point ☐Split Key Used: ☐ 1 ☐ 2 ☐ 3 ☐ 4 ☐ 5 ☐ 6 ☐ 7	_____

Account: _____	Additional Notes:
Username: _____	_____
Password: _____	_____
Secret Key: ☐Start ☐End ☐Middle ☐Indicated Point ☐Split Key Used: ☐ 1 ☐ 2 ☐ 3 ☐ 4 ☐ 5 ☐ 6 ☐ 7	_____

Account: _____	Additional Notes:
Username: _____	_____
Password: _____	_____
Secret Key: ☐Start ☐End ☐Middle ☐Indicated Point ☐Split Key Used: ☐ 1 ☐ 2 ☐ 3 ☐ 4 ☐ 5 ☐ 6 ☐ 7	_____

Account: _____	Additional Notes:
Username: _____	_____
Password: _____	_____
Secret Key: ☐Start ☐End ☐Middle ☐Indicated Point ☐Split Key Used: ☐ 1 ☐ 2 ☐ 3 ☐ 4 ☐ 5 ☐ 6 ☐ 7	_____

The Encrypted Book of Passwords

Account: _____   Additional Notes:

Username: _____   _____

Password: _____   _____

Secret Key: □Start □End □Middle □Indicated Point □Split   _____
Key Used: □1 □2 □3 □4 □5 □6 □7

Account: _____   Additional Notes:

Username: _____   _____

Password: _____   _____

Secret Key: □Start □End □Middle □Indicated Point □Split   _____
Key Used: □1 □2 □3 □4 □5 □6 □7

Account: _____   Additional Notes:

Username: _____   _____

Password: _____   _____

Secret Key: □Start □End □Middle □Indicated Point □Split   _____
Key Used: □1 □2 □3 □4 □5 □6 □7

Account: _____   Additional Notes:

Username: _____   _____

Password: _____   _____

Secret Key: □Start □End □Middle □Indicated Point □Split   _____
Key Used: □1 □2 □3 □4 □5 □6 □7

Account: _____   Additional Notes:

Username: _____   _____

Password: _____   _____

Secret Key: □Start □End □Middle □Indicated Point □Split   _____
Key Used: □1 □2 □3 □4 □5 □6 □7

B

Account: _____	Additional Notes:
Username: _____	_____
Password: _____	_____
Secret Key: ☐Start ☐End ☐Middle ☐Indicated Point ☐Split Key Used: ☐1 ☐2 ☐3 ☐4 ☐5 ☐6 ☐7	_____

Account: _____	Additional Notes:
Username: _____	_____
Password: _____	_____
Secret Key: ☐Start ☐End ☐Middle ☐Indicated Point ☐Split Key Used: ☐1 ☐2 ☐3 ☐4 ☐5 ☐6 ☐7	_____

Account: _____	Additional Notes:
Username: _____	_____
Password: _____	_____
Secret Key: ☐Start ☐End ☐Middle ☐Indicated Point ☐Split Key Used: ☐1 ☐2 ☐3 ☐4 ☐5 ☐6 ☐7	_____

Account: _____	Additional Notes:
Username: _____	_____
Password: _____	_____
Secret Key: ☐Start ☐End ☐Middle ☐Indicated Point ☐Split Key Used: ☐1 ☐2 ☐3 ☐4 ☐5 ☐6 ☐7	_____

Account: _____	Additional Notes:
Username: _____	_____
Password: _____	_____
Secret Key: ☐Start ☐End ☐Middle ☐Indicated Point ☐Split Key Used: ☐1 ☐2 ☐3 ☐4 ☐5 ☐6 ☐7	_____

Account: _____ Additional Notes:

Username: _____ _____

Password: _____ _____

Secret Key: ☐Start ☐End ☐Middle ☐Indicated Point ☐Split _____
Key Used: ☐ 1 ☐ 2 ☐ 3 ☐ 4 ☐ 5 ☐ 6 ☐ 7

Account: _____ Additional Notes:

Username: _____ _____

Password: _____ _____

Secret Key: ☐Start ☐End ☐Middle ☐Indicated Point ☐Split _____
Key Used: ☐ 1 ☐ 2 ☐ 3 ☐ 4 ☐ 5 ☐ 6 ☐ 7

Account: _____ Additional Notes:

Username: _____ _____

Password: _____ _____

Secret Key: ☐Start ☐End ☐Middle ☐Indicated Point ☐Split _____
Key Used: ☐ 1 ☐ 2 ☐ 3 ☐ 4 ☐ 5 ☐ 6 ☐ 7

Account: _____ Additional Notes:

Username: _____ _____

Password: _____ _____

Secret Key: ☐Start ☐End ☐Middle ☐Indicated Point ☐Split _____
Key Used: ☐ 1 ☐ 2 ☐ 3 ☐ 4 ☐ 5 ☐ 6 ☐ 7

Account: _____ Additional Notes:

Username: _____ _____

Password: _____ _____

Secret Key: ☐Start ☐End ☐Middle ☐Indicated Point ☐Split _____
Key Used: ☐ 1 ☐ 2 ☐ 3 ☐ 4 ☐ 5 ☐ 6 ☐ 7

Account: _____	Additional Notes:
Username: _____	_____
Password: _____	_____
Secret Key: ☐Start ☐End ☐Middle ☐Indicated Point ☐Split Key Used: ☐ 1 ☐ 2 ☐ 3 ☐ 4 ☐ 5 ☐ 6 ☐ 7	_____

Account: _____	Additional Notes:
Username: _____	_____
Password: _____	_____
Secret Key: ☐Start ☐End ☐Middle ☐Indicated Point ☐Split Key Used: ☐ 1 ☐ 2 ☐ 3 ☐ 4 ☐ 5 ☐ 6 ☐ 7	_____

Account: _____	Additional Notes:
Username: _____	_____
Password: _____	_____
Secret Key: ☐Start ☐End ☐Middle ☐Indicated Point ☐Split Key Used: ☐ 1 ☐ 2 ☐ 3 ☐ 4 ☐ 5 ☐ 6 ☐ 7	_____

Account: _____	Additional Notes:
Username: _____	_____
Password: _____	_____
Secret Key: ☐Start ☐End ☐Middle ☐Indicated Point ☐Split Key Used: ☐ 1 ☐ 2 ☐ 3 ☐ 4 ☐ 5 ☐ 6 ☐ 7	_____

Account: _____	Additional Notes.
Username: _____	_____
Password: _____	_____
Secret Key: ☐Start ☐End ☐Middle ☐Indicated Point ☐Split Key Used: ☐ 1 ☐ 2 ☐ 3 ☐ 4 ☐ 5 ☐ 6 ☐ 7	_____

The Encrypted Book of Passwords

Account: _____	Additional Notes:
Username: _____	_____
Password: _____	_____
Secret Key: ☐Start ☐End ☐Middle ☐Indicated Point ☐Split Key Used: ☐1 ☐2 ☐3 ☐4 ☐5 ☐6 ☐7	_____

Account: _____	Additional Notes:
Username: _____	_____
Password: _____	_____
Secret Key: ☐Start ☐End ☐Middle ☐Indicated Point ☐Split Key Used: ☐1 ☐2 ☐3 ☐4 ☐5 ☐6 ☐7	_____

Account: _____	Additional Notes:
Username: _____	_____
Password: _____	_____
Secret Key: ☐Start ☐End ☐Middle ☐Indicated Point ☐Split Key Used: ☐1 ☐2 ☐3 ☐4 ☐5 ☐6 ☐7	_____

Account: _____	Additional Notes:
Username: _____	_____
Password: _____	_____
Secret Key: ☐Start ☐End ☐Middle ☐Indicated Point ☐Split Key Used: ☐1 ☐2 ☐3 ☐4 ☐5 ☐6 ☐7	_____

Account: _____	Additional Notes:
Username: _____	_____
Password: _____	_____
Secret Key: ☐Start ☐End ☐Middle ☐Indicated Point ☐Split Key Used: ☐1 ☐2 ☐3 ☐4 ☐5 ☐6 ☐7	_____

C

Account: _____	Additional Notes:
Username: _____	_____
Password: _____	_____
Secret Key: ☐Start ☐End ☐Middle ☐Indicated Point ☐Split Key Used: ☐ 1 ☐ 2 ☐ 3 ☐ 4 ☐ 5 ☐ 6 ☐ 7	_____

Account: _____	Additional Notes:
Username: _____	_____
Password: _____	_____
Secret Key: ☐Start ☐End ☐Middle ☐Indicated Point ☐Split Key Used: ☐ 1 ☐ 2 ☐ 3 ☐ 4 ☐ 5 ☐ 6 ☐ 7	_____

Account: _____	Additional Notes:
Username: _____	_____
Password: _____	_____
Secret Key: ☐Start ☐End ☐Middle ☐Indicated Point ☐Split Key Used: ☐ 1 ☐ 2 ☐ 3 ☐ 4 ☐ 5 ☐ 6 ☐ 7	_____

Account: _____	Additional Notes:
Username: _____	_____
Password: _____	_____
Secret Key: ☐Start ☐End ☐Middle ☐Indicated Point ☐Split Key Used: ☐ 1 ☐ 2 ☐ 3 ☐ 4 ☐ 5 ☐ 6 ☐ 7	_____

Account: _____	Additional Notes:
Username: _____	_____
Password: _____	_____
Secret Key: ☐Start ☐End ☐Middle ☐Indicated Point ☐Split Key Used: ☐ 1 ☐ 2 ☐ 3 ☐ 4 ☐ 5 ☐ 6 ☐ 7	_____

Account: _____	Additional Notes:
Username: _____	_____
Password: _____	_____
Secret Key: ☐Start ☐End ☐Middle ☐Indicated Point ☐Split Key Used: ☐ 1 ☐ 2 ☐ 3 ☐ 4 ☐ 5 ☐ 6 ☐ 7	_____

Account: _____	Additional Notes:
Username: _____	_____
Password: _____	_____
Secret Key: ☐Start ☐End ☐Middle ☐Indicated Point ☐Split Key Used: ☐ 1 ☐ 2 ☐ 3 ☐ 4 ☐ 5 ☐ 6 ☐ 7	_____

Account: _____	Additional Notes:
Username: _____	_____
Password: _____	_____
Secret Key: ☐Start ☐End ☐Middle ☐Indicated Point ☐Split Key Used: ☐ 1 ☐ 2 ☐ 3 ☐ 4 ☐ 5 ☐ 6 ☐ 7	_____

Account: _____	Additional Notes:
Username: _____	_____
Password: _____	_____
Secret Key: ☐Start ☐End ☐Middle ☐Indicated Point ☐Split Key Used: ☐ 1 ☐ 2 ☐ 3 ☐ 4 ☐ 5 ☐ 6 ☐ 7	_____

Account: _____	Additional Notes:
Username: _____	_____
Password: _____	_____
Secret Key: ☐Start ☐End ☐Middle ☐Indicated Point ☐Split Key Used: ☐ 1 ☐ 2 ☐ 3 ☐ 4 ☐ 5 ☐ 6 ☐ 7	_____

Account: _____   Additional Notes:

Username: _____   _____

Password: _____   _____

Secret Key: ☐Start ☐End ☐Middle ☐Indicated Point ☐Split
Key Used: ☐ 1 ☐ 2 ☐ 3 ☐ 4 ☐ 5 ☐ 6 ☐ 7   _____

Account: _____   Additional Notes:

Username: _____   _____

Password: _____   _____

Secret Key: ☐Start ☐End ☐Middle ☐Indicated Point ☐Split
Key Used: ☐ 1 ☐ 2 ☐ 3 ☐ 4 ☐ 5 ☐ 6 ☐ 7   _____

Account: _____   Additional Notes:

Username: _____   _____

Password: _____   _____

Secret Key: ☐Start ☐End ☐Middle ☐Indicated Point ☐Split
Key Used: ☐ 1 ☐ 2 ☐ 3 ☐ 4 ☐ 5 ☐ 6 ☐ 7   _____

Account: _____   Additional Notes:

Username: _____   _____

Password: _____   _____

Secret Key: ☐Start ☐End ☐Middle ☐Indicated Point ☐Split
Key Used: ☐ 1 ☐ 2 ☐ 3 ☐ 4 ☐ 5 ☐ 6 ☐ 7   _____

Account: _____   Additional Notes:

Username: _____   _____

Password: _____   _____

Secret Key: ☐Start ☐End ☐Middle ☐Indicated Point ☐Split
Key Used: ☐ 1 ☐ 2 ☐ 3 ☐ 4 ☐ 5 ☐ 6 ☐ 7   _____

The Encrypted Book of Passwords

Account: _____   Additional Notes:

Username: _____   _____

Password: _____   _____

Secret Key: ☐Start ☐End ☐Middle ☐Indicated Point ☐Split   _____
Key Used: ☐ 1 ☐ 2 ☐ 3 ☐ 4 ☐ 5 ☐ 6 ☐ 7

Account: _____   Additional Notes:

Username: _____   _____

Password: _____   _____

Secret Key: ☐Start ☐End ☐Middle ☐Indicated Point ☐Split   _____
Key Used: ☐ 1 ☐ 2 ☐ 3 ☐ 4 ☐ 5 ☐ 6 ☐ 7

Account: _____   Additional Notes:

Username: _____   _____

Password: _____   _____

Secret Key: ☐Start ☐End ☐Middle ☐Indicated Point ☐Split   _____
Key Used: ☐ 1 ☐ 2 ☐ 3 ☐ 4 ☐ 5 ☐ 6 ☐ 7

Account: _____   Additional Notes:

Username: _____   _____

Password: _____   _____

Secret Key: ☐Start ☐End ☐Middle ☐Indicated Point ☐Split   _____
Key Used: ☐ 1 ☐ 2 ☐ 3 ☐ 4 ☐ 5 ☐ 6 ☐ 7

Account: _____   Additional Notes:

Username: _____   _____

Password: _____   _____

Secret Key: ☐Start ☐End ☐Middle ☐Indicated Point ☐Split   _____
Key Used: ☐ 1 ☐ 2 ☐ 3 ☐ 4 ☐ 5 ☐ 6 ☐ 7

D

Account: _____   Additional Notes:

Username: _____   _____

Password: _____   _____

Secret Key: □Start □End □Middle □Indicated Point □Split   _____
Key Used: □ 1 □ 2 □ 3 □ 4 □ 5 □ 6 □ 7

Account: _____   Additional Notes:

Username: _____   _____

Password: _____   _____

Secret Key: □Start □End □Middle □Indicated Point □Split   _____
Key Used: □ 1 □ 2 □ 3 □ 4 □ 5 □ 6 □ 7

Account: _____   Additional Notes:

Username: _____   _____

Password: _____   _____

Secret Key: □Start □End □Middle □Indicated Point □Split   _____
Key Used: □ 1 □ 2 □ 3 □ 4 □ 5 □ 6 □ 7

Account: _____   Additional Notes:

Username: _____   _____

Password: _____   _____

Secret Key: □Start □End □Middle □Indicated Point □Split   _____
Key Used: □ 1 □ 2 □ 3 □ 4 □ 5 □ 6 □ 7

Account: _____   Additional Notes:

Username: _____   _____

Password: _____   _____

Secret Key: □Start □End □Middle □Indicated Point □Split   _____
Key Used: □ 1 □ 2 □ 3 □ 4 □ 5 □ 6 □ 7

Account: _____   Additional Notes:

Username: _____   _____

Password: _____   _____

Secret Key: ☐Start ☐End ☐Middle ☐Indicated Point ☐Split   _____
Key Used: ☐ 1 ☐ 2 ☐ 3 ☐ 4 ☐ 5 ☐ 6 ☐ 7

Account: _____   Additional Notes:

Username: _____   _____

Password: _____   _____

Secret Key: ☐Start ☐End ☐Middle ☐Indicated Point ☐Split   _____
Key Used: ☐ 1 ☐ 2 ☐ 3 ☐ 4 ☐ 5 ☐ 6 ☐ 7

Account: _____   Additional Notes:

Username: _____   _____

Password: _____   _____

Secret Key: ☐Start ☐End ☐Middle ☐Indicated Point ☐Split   _____
Key Used: ☐ 1 ☐ 2 ☐ 3 ☐ 4 ☐ 5 ☐ 6 ☐ 7

Account: _____   Additional Notes:

Username: _____   _____

Password: _____   _____

Secret Key: ☐Start ☐End ☐Middle ☐Indicated Point ☐Split   _____
Key Used: ☐ 1 ☐ 2 ☐ 3 ☐ 4 ☐ 5 ☐ 6 ☐ 7

Account: _____   Additional Notes:

Username: _____   _____

Password: _____   _____

Secret Key: ☐Start ☐End ☐Middle ☐Indicated Point ☐Split   _____
Key Used: ☐ 1 ☐ 2 ☐ 3 ☐ 4 ☐ 5 ☐ 6 ☐ 7

Account: _____	Additional Notes:
Username: _____	_____
Password: _____	_____
Secret Key: □Start □End □Middle □Indicated Point □Split Key Used: □ 1 □ 2 □ 3 □ 4 □ 5 □ 6 □ 7	_____

Account: _____	Additional Notes:
Username: _____	_____
Password: _____	_____
Secret Key: □Start □End □Middle □Indicated Point □Split Key Used: □ 1 □ 2 □ 3 □ 4 □ 5 □ 6 □ 7	_____

Account: _____	Additional Notes:
Username: _____	_____
Password: _____	_____
Secret Key: □Start □End □Middle □Indicated Point □Split Key Used: □ 1 □ 2 □ 3 □ 4 □ 5 □ 6 □ 7	_____

Account: _____	Additional Notes:
Username: _____	_____
Password: _____	_____
Secret Key: □Start □End □Middle □Indicated Point □Split Key Used: □ 1 □ 2 □ 3 □ 4 □ 5 □ 6 □ 7	_____

Account: _____	Additional Notes:
Username: _____	_____
Password: _____	_____
Secret Key: □Start □End □Middle □Indicated Point □Split Key Used: □ 1 □ 2 □ 3 □ 4 □ 5 □ 6 □ 7	_____

Account: _____ Additional Notes:

Username: _____ _____

Password: _____ _____

Secret Key: ☐Start ☐End ☐Middle ☐Indicated Point ☐Split _____
Key Used: ☐ 1 ☐ 2 ☐ 3 ☐ 4 ☐ 5 ☐ 6 ☐ 7

Account: _____ Additional Notes:

Username: _____ _____

Password: _____ _____

Secret Key: ☐Start ☐End ☐Middle ☐Indicated Point ☐Split _____
Key Used: ☐ 1 ☐ 2 ☐ 3 ☐ 4 ☐ 5 ☐ 6 ☐ 7

Account: _____ Additional Notes:

Username: _____ _____

Password: _____ _____

Secret Key: ☐Start ☐End ☐Middle ☐Indicated Point ☐Split _____
Key Used: ☐ 1 ☐ 2 ☐ 3 ☐ 4 ☐ 5 ☐ 6 ☐ 7

Account: _____ Additional Notes:

Username: _____ _____

Password: _____ _____

Secret Key: ☐Start ☐End ☐Middle ☐Indicated Point ☐Split _____
Key Used: ☐ 1 ☐ 2 ☐ 3 ☐ 4 ☐ 5 ☐ 6 ☐ 7

Account: _____ Additional Notes:

Username: _____ _____

Password: _____ _____

Secret Key: ☐Start ☐End ☐Middle ☐Indicated Point ☐Split _____
Key Used: ☐ 1 ☐ 2 ☐ 3 ☐ 4 ☐ 5 ☐ 6 ☐ 7

E

Account: _____	Additional Notes:
Username: _____	_____
Password: _____	_____
Secret Key: ☐Start ☐End ☐Middle ☐Indicated Point ☐Split Key Used: ☐ 1 ☐ 2 ☐ 3 ☐ 4 ☐ 5 ☐ 6 ☐ 7	_____

Account: _____	Additional Notes:
Username: _____	_____
Password: _____	_____
Secret Key: ☐Start ☐End ☐Middle ☐Indicated Point ☐Split Key Used: ☐ 1 ☐ 2 ☐ 3 ☐ 4 ☐ 5 ☐ 6 ☐ 7	_____

Account: _____	Additional Notes:
Username: _____	_____
Password: _____	_____
Secret Key: ☐Start ☐End ☐Middle ☐Indicated Point ☐Split Key Used: ☐ 1 ☐ 2 ☐ 3 ☐ 4 ☐ 5 ☐ 6 ☐ 7	_____

Account: _____	Additional Notes:
Username: _____	_____
Password: _____	_____
Secret Key: ☐Start ☐End ☐Middle ☐Indicated Point ☐Split Key Used: ☐ 1 ☐ 2 ☐ 3 ☐ 4 ☐ 5 ☐ 6 ☐ 7	_____

Account: _____	Additional Notes:
Username: _____	_____
Password: _____	_____
Secret Key: ☐Start ☐End ☐Middle ☐Indicated Point ☐Split Key Used: ☐ 1 ☐ 2 ☐ 3 ☐ 4 ☐ 5 ☐ 6 ☐ 7	_____

Account: _____ Additional Notes:

Username: _____ _____

Password: _____ _____

Secret Key: □Start □End □Middle □Indicated Point □Split _____
Key Used: □ 1 □ 2 □ 3 □ 4 □ 5 □ 6 □ 7

Account: _____ Additional Notes:

Username: _____ _____

Password: _____ _____

Secret Key: □Start □End □Middle □Indicated Point □Split _____
Key Used: □ 1 □ 2 □ 3 □ 4 □ 5 □ 6 □ 7

Account: _____ Additional Notes:

Username: _____ _____

Password: _____ _____

Secret Key: □Start □End □Middle □Indicated Point □Split _____
Key Used: □ 1 □ 2 □ 3 □ 4 □ 5 □ 6 □ 7

Account: _____ Additional Notes:

Username: _____ _____

Password: _____ _____

Secret Key: □Start □End □Middle □Indicated Point □Split _____
Key Used: □ 1 □ 2 □ 3 □ 4 □ 5 □ 6 □ 7

Account: _____ Additional Notes:

Username: _____ _____

Password: _____ _____

Secret Key: □Start □End □Middle □Indicated Point □Split _____
Key Used: □ 1 □ 2 □ 3 □ 4 □ 5 □ 6 □ 7

Account: _____	Additional Notes:
Username: _____	_____
Password: _____	_____
Secret Key: ☐Start ☐End ☐Middle ☐Indicated Point ☐Split Key Used: ☐1 ☐2 ☐3 ☐4 ☐5 ☐6 ☐7	_____

Account: _____	Additional Notes:
Username: _____	_____
Password: _____	_____
Secret Key: ☐Start ☐End ☐Middle ☐Indicated Point ☐Split Key Used: ☐1 ☐2 ☐3 ☐4 ☐5 ☐6 ☐7	_____

Account: _____	Additional Notes:
Username: _____	_____
Password: _____	_____
Secret Key: ☐Start ☐End ☐Middle ☐Indicated Point ☐Split Key Used: ☐1 ☐2 ☐3 ☐4 ☐5 ☐6 ☐7	_____

Account: _____	Additional Notes:
Username: _____	_____
Password: _____	_____
Secret Key: ☐Start ☐End ☐Middle ☐Indicated Point ☐Split Key Used: ☐1 ☐2 ☐3 ☐4 ☐5 ☐6 ☐7	_____

Account: _____	Additional Notes:
Username: _____	_____
Password: _____	_____
Secret Key: ☐Start ☐End ☐Middle ☐Indicated Point ☐Split Key Used: ☐1 ☐2 ☐3 ☐4 ☐5 ☐6 ☐7	_____

Account: _____   Additional Notes:

Username: _____   _____

Password: _____   _____

Secret Key: ☐Start ☐End ☐Middle ☐Indicated Point ☐Split   _____
Key Used: ☐ 1 ☐ 2 ☐ 3 ☐ 4 ☐ 5 ☐ 6 ☐ 7

Account: _____   Additional Notes:

Username: _____   _____

Password: _____   _____

Secret Key: ☐Start ☐End ☐Middle ☐Indicated Point ☐Split   _____
Key Used: ☐ 1 ☐ 2 ☐ 3 ☐ 4 ☐ 5 ☐ 6 ☐ 7

Account: _____   Additional Notes:

Username: _____   _____

Password: _____   _____

Secret Key: ☐Start ☐End ☐Middle ☐Indicated Point ☐Split   _____
Key Used: ☐ 1 ☐ 2 ☐ 3 ☐ 4 ☐ 5 ☐ 6 ☐ 7

Account: _____   Additional Notes:

Username: _____   _____

Password: _____   _____

Secret Key: ☐Start ☐End ☐Middle ☐Indicated Point ☐Split   _____
Key Used: ☐ 1 ☐ 2 ☐ 3 ☐ 4 ☐ 5 ☐ 6 ☐ 7

Account: _____   Additional Notes:

Username: _____   _____

Password: _____   _____

Secret Key: ☐Start ☐End ☐Middle ☐Indicated Point ☐Split   _____
Key Used: ☐ 1 ☐ 2 ☐ 3 ☐ 4 ☐ 5 ☐ 6 ☐ 7

F

Account: _____	Additional Notes:
Username: _____	_____
Password: _____	_____
Secret Key: ☐Start ☐End ☐Middle ☐Indicated Point ☐Split	_____
Key Used: ☐ 1 ☐ 2 ☐ 3 ☐ 4 ☐ 5 ☐ 6 ☐ 7	

Account: _____	Additional Notes:
Username: _____	_____
Password: _____	_____
Secret Key: ☐Start ☐End ☐Middle ☐Indicated Point ☐Split	_____
Key Used: ☐ 1 ☐ 2 ☐ 3 ☐ 4 ☐ 5 ☐ 6 ☐ 7	

Account: _____	Additional Notes:
Username: _____	_____
Password: _____	_____
Secret Key: ☐Start ☐End ☐Middle ☐Indicated Point ☐Split	_____
Key Used: ☐ 1 ☐ 2 ☐ 3 ☐ 4 ☐ 5 ☐ 6 ☐ 7	

Account: _____	Additional Notes:
Username: _____	_____
Password: _____	_____
Secret Key: ☐Start ☐End ☐Middle ☐Indicated Point ☐Split	_____
Key Used: ☐ 1 ☐ 2 ☐ 3 ☐ 4 ☐ 5 ☐ 6 ☐ 7	

Account: _____	Additional Notes:
Username: _____	_____
Password: _____	_____
Secret Key: ☐Start ☐End ☐Middle ☐Indicated Point ☐Split	_____
Key Used: ☐ 1 ☐ 2 ☐ 3 ☐ 4 ☐ 5 ☐ 6 ☐ 7	

Account: _____   Additional Notes:

Username: _____   _____

Password: _____   _____

Secret Key: ☐Start ☐End ☐Middle ☐Indicated Point ☐Split   _____
Key Used: ☐ 1 ☐ 2 ☐ 3 ☐ 4 ☐ 5 ☐ 6 ☐ 7

Account: _____   Additional Notes:

Username: _____   _____

Password: _____   _____

Secret Key: ☐Start ☐End ☐Middle ☐Indicated Point ☐Split   _____
Key Used: ☐ 1 ☐ 2 ☐ 3 ☐ 4 ☐ 5 ☐ 6 ☐ 7

Account: _____   Additional Notes:

Username: _____   _____

Password: _____   _____

Secret Key: ☐Start ☐End ☐Middle ☐Indicated Point ☐Split   _____
Key Used: ☐ 1 ☐ 2 ☐ 3 ☐ 4 ☐ 5 ☐ 6 ☐ 7

Account: _____   Additional Notes:

Username: _____   _____

Password: _____   _____

Secret Key: ☐Start ☐End ☐Middle ☐Indicated Point ☐Split   _____
Key Used: ☐ 1 ☐ 2 ☐ 3 ☐ 4 ☐ 5 ☐ 6 ☐ 7

Account: _____   Additional Notes:

Username: _____   _____

Password: _____   _____

Secret Key: ☐Start ☐End ☐Middle ☐Indicated Point ☐Split   _____
Key Used: ☐ 1 ☐ 2 ☐ 3 ☐ 4 ☐ 5 ☐ 6 ☐ 7

Account: _____   Additional Notes:

Username: _____   _____

Password: _____   _____

Secret Key: ☐Start ☐End ☐Middle ☐Indicated Point ☐Split
Key Used: ☐ 1 ☐ 2 ☐ 3 ☐ 4 ☐ 5 ☐ 6 ☐ 7   _____

Account: _____   Additional Notes:

Username: _____   _____

Password: _____   _____

Secret Key: ☐Start ☐End ☐Middle ☐Indicated Point ☐Split
Key Used: ☐ 1 ☐ 2 ☐ 3 ☐ 4 ☐ 5 ☐ 6 ☐ 7   _____

Account: _____   Additional Notes:

Username: _____   _____

Password: _____   _____

Secret Key: ☐Start ☐End ☐Middle ☐Indicated Point ☐Split
Key Used: ☐ 1 ☐ 2 ☐ 3 ☐ 4 ☐ 5 ☐ 6 ☐ 7   _____

Account: _____   Additional Notes:

Username: _____   _____

Password: _____   _____

Secret Key: ☐Start ☐End ☐Middle ☐Indicated Point ☐Split
Key Used: ☐ 1 ☐ 2 ☐ 3 ☐ 4 ☐ 5 ☐ 6 ☐ 7   _____

Account: _____   Additional Notes:

Username: _____   _____

Password: _____   _____

Secret Key: ☐Start ☐End ☐Middle ☐Indicated Point ☐Split
Key Used: ☐ 1 ☐ 2 ☐ 3 ☐ 4 ☐ 5 ☐ 6 ☐ 7   _____

The Encrypted Book of Passwords

Account: _____   Additional Notes:

Username: _____

Password: _____   _____

Secret Key: ☐Start ☐End ☐Middle ☐Indicated Point ☐Split
Key Used: ☐ 1 ☐ 2 ☐ 3 ☐ 4 ☐ 5 ☐ 6 ☐ 7   _____

Account: _____   Additional Notes:

Username: _____

Password: _____   _____

Secret Key: ☐Start ☐End ☐Middle ☐Indicated Point ☐Split
Key Used: ☐ 1 ☐ 2 ☐ 3 ☐ 4 ☐ 5 ☐ 6 ☐ 7   _____

Account: _____   Additional Notes:

Username: _____

Password: _____   _____

Secret Key: ☐Start ☐End ☐Middle ☐Indicated Point ☐Split
Key Used: ☐ 1 ☐ 2 ☐ 3 ☐ 4 ☐ 5 ☐ 6 ☐ 7   _____

Account: _____   Additional Notes:

Username: _____

Password: _____   _____

Secret Key: ☐Start ☐End ☐Middle ☐Indicated Point ☐Split
Key Used: ☐ 1 ☐ 2 ☐ 3 ☐ 4 ☐ 5 ☐ 6 ☐ 7   _____

Account: _____   Additional Notes:

Username: _____

Password: _____   _____

Secret Key: ☐Start ☐End ☐Middle ☐Indicated Point ☐Split
Key Used: ☐ 1 ☐ 2 ☐ 3 ☐ 4 ☐ 5 ☐ 6 ☐ 7   _____

G

Account: _____ Additional Notes:

Username: _____ _____

Password: _____ _____

Secret Key: ☐Start ☐End ☐Middle ☐Indicated Point ☐Split _____
Key Used: ☐ 1 ☐ 2 ☐ 3 ☐ 4 ☐ 5 ☐ 6 ☐ 7

Account: _____ Additional Notes:

Username: _____ _____

Password: _____ _____

Secret Key: ☐Start ☐End ☐Middle ☐Indicated Point ☐Split _____
Key Used: ☐ 1 ☐ 2 ☐ 3 ☐ 4 ☐ 5 ☐ 6 ☐ 7

Account: _____ Additional Notes:

Username: _____ _____

Password: _____ _____

Secret Key: ☐Start ☐End ☐Middle ☐Indicated Point ☐Split _____
Key Used: ☐ 1 ☐ 2 ☐ 3 ☐ 4 ☐ 5 ☐ 6 ☐ 7

Account: _____ Additional Notes:

Username: _____ _____

Password: _____ _____

Secret Key: ☐Start ☐End ☐Middle ☐Indicated Point ☐Split _____
Key Used: ☐ 1 ☐ 2 ☐ 3 ☐ 4 ☐ 5 ☐ 6 ☐ 7

Account: _____ Additional Notes:

Username: _____ _____

Password: _____ _____

Secret Key: ☐Start ☐End ☐Middle ☐Indicated Point ☐Split _____
Key Used: ☐ 1 ☐ 2 ☐ 3 ☐ 4 ☐ 5 ☐ 6 ☐ 7

The Encrypted Book of Passwords

Account: _____   Additional Notes:

Username: _____   _____

Password: _____   _____

Secret Key: ☐Start ☐End ☐Middle ☐Indicated Point ☐Split   _____
Key Used: ☐ 1 ☐ 2 ☐ 3 ☐ 4 ☐ 5 ☐ 6 ☐ 7

Account: _____   Additional Notes:

Username: _____   _____

Password: _____   _____

Secret Key: ☐Start ☐End ☐Middle ☐Indicated Point ☐Split   _____
Key Used: ☐ 1 ☐ 2 ☐ 3 ☐ 4 ☐ 5 ☐ 6 ☐ 7

Account: _____   Additional Notes:

Username: _____   _____

Password: _____   _____

Secret Key: ☐Start ☐End ☐Middle ☐Indicated Point ☐Split   _____
Key Used: ☐ 1 ☐ 2 ☐ 3 ☐ 4 ☐ 5 ☐ 6 ☐ 7

Account: _____   Additional Notes:

Username: _____   _____

Password: _____   _____

Secret Key: ☐Start ☐End ☐Middle ☐Indicated Point ☐Split   _____
Key Used: ☐ 1 ☐ 2 ☐ 3 ☐ 4 ☐ 5 ☐ 6 ☐ 7

Account: _____   Additional Notes:

Username: _____   _____

Password: _____   _____

Secret Key: ☐Start ☐End ☐Middle ☐Indicated Point ☐Split   _____
Key Used: ☐ 1 ☐ 2 ☐ 3 ☐ 4 ☐ 5 ☐ 6 ☐ 7

Account: _____	Additional Notes:
Username: _____	_____
Password: _____	_____
Secret Key: ☐Start ☐End ☐Middle ☐Indicated Point ☐Split Key Used: ☐1 ☐2 ☐3 ☐4 ☐5 ☐6 ☐7	_____

Account: _____	Additional Notes:
Username: _____	_____
Password: _____	_____
Secret Key: ☐Start ☐End ☐Middle ☐Indicated Point ☐Split Key Used: ☐1 ☐2 ☐3 ☐4 ☐5 ☐6 ☐7	_____

Account: _____	Additional Notes:
Username: _____	_____
Password: _____	_____
Secret Key: ☐Start ☐End ☐Middle ☐Indicated Point ☐Split Key Used: ☐1 ☐2 ☐3 ☐4 ☐5 ☐6 ☐7	_____

Account: _____	Additional Notes:
Username: _____	_____
Password: _____	_____
Secret Key: ☐Start ☐End ☐Middle ☐Indicated Point ☐Split Key Used: ☐1 ☐2 ☐3 ☐4 ☐5 ☐6 ☐7	_____

Account: _____	Additional Notes:
Username: _____	_____
Password: _____	_____
Secret Key: ☐Start ☐End ☐Middle ☐Indicated Point ☐Split Key Used: ☐1 ☐2 ☐3 ☐4 ☐5 ☐6 ☐7	_____

Account: _____   Additional Notes:

Username: _____   _____

Password: _____   _____

Secret Key: ☐Start ☐End ☐Middle ☐Indicated Point ☐Split   _____
Key Used: ☐ 1 ☐ 2 ☐ 3 ☐ 4 ☐ 5 ☐ 6 ☐ 7

Account: _____   Additional Notes:

Username: _____   _____

Password: _____   _____

Secret Key: ☐Start ☐End ☐Middle ☐Indicated Point ☐Split   _____
Key Used: ☐ 1 ☐ 2 ☐ 3 ☐ 4 ☐ 5 ☐ 6 ☐ 7

Account: _____   Additional Notes:

Username: _____   _____

Password: _____   _____

Secret Key: ☐Start ☐End ☐Middle ☐Indicated Point ☐Split   _____
Key Used: ☐ 1 ☐ 2 ☐ 3 ☐ 4 ☐ 5 ☐ 6 ☐ 7

Account: _____   Additional Notes:

Username: _____   _____

Password: _____   _____

Secret Key: ☐Start ☐End ☐Middle ☐Indicated Point ☐Split   _____
Key Used: ☐ 1 ☐ 2 ☐ 3 ☐ 4 ☐ 5 ☐ 6 ☐ 7

Account: _____   Additional Notes:

Username: _____   _____

Password: _____   _____

Secret Key: ☐Start ☐End ☐Middle ☐Indicated Point ☐Split   _____
Key Used: ☐ 1 ☐ 2 ☐ 3 ☐ 4 ☐ 5 ☐ 6 ☐ 7

H

Account: _____	Additional Notes:
Username: _____	_____
Password: _____	_____
Secret Key: ☐Start ☐End ☐Middle ☐Indicated Point ☐Split Key Used: ☐ 1 ☐ 2 ☐ 3 ☐ 4 ☐ 5 ☐ 6 ☐ 7	_____

Account: _____	Additional Notes:
Username: _____	_____
Password: _____	_____
Secret Key: ☐Start ☐End ☐Middle ☐Indicated Point ☐Split Key Used: ☐ 1 ☐ 2 ☐ 3 ☐ 4 ☐ 5 ☐ 6 ☐ 7	_____

Account: _____	Additional Notes:
Username: _____	_____
Password: _____	_____
Secret Key: ☐Start ☐End ☐Middle ☐Indicated Point ☐Split Key Used: ☐ 1 ☐ 2 ☐ 3 ☐ 4 ☐ 5 ☐ 6 ☐ 7	_____

Account: _____	Additional Notes:
Username: _____	_____
Password: _____	_____
Secret Key: ☐Start ☐End ☐Middle ☐Indicated Point ☐Split Key Used: ☐ 1 ☐ 2 ☐ 3 ☐ 4 ☐ 5 ☐ 6 ☐ 7	_____

Account: _____	Additional Notes:
Username: _____	_____
Password: _____	_____
Secret Key: ☐Start ☐End ☐Middle ☐Indicated Point ☐Split Key Used: ☐ 1 ☐ 2 ☐ 3 ☐ 4 ☐ 5 ☐ 6 ☐ 7	_____

The Encrypted Book of Passwords

Account: _____   Additional Notes:

Username: _____

Password: _____   _____

Secret Key: ☐Start ☐End ☐Middle ☐Indicated Point ☐Split
Key Used: ☐ 1 ☐ 2 ☐ 3 ☐ 4 ☐ 5 ☐ 6 ☐ 7   _____

Account: _____   Additional Notes:

Username: _____

Password: _____   _____

Secret Key: ☐Start ☐End ☐Middle ☐Indicated Point ☐Split
Key Used: ☐ 1 ☐ 2 ☐ 3 ☐ 4 ☐ 5 ☐ 6 ☐ 7   _____

Account: _____   Additional Notes:

Username: _____

Password: _____   _____

Secret Key: ☐Start ☐End ☐Middle ☐Indicated Point ☐Split
Key Used: ☐ 1 ☐ 2 ☐ 3 ☐ 4 ☐ 5 ☐ 6 ☐ 7   _____

Account: _____   Additional Notes:

Username: _____

Password: _____   _____

Secret Key: ☐Start ☐End ☐Middle ☐Indicated Point ☐Split
Key Used: ☐ 1 ☐ 2 ☐ 3 ☐ 4 ☐ 5 ☐ 6 ☐ 7   _____

Account: _____   Additional Notes:

Username: _____

Password: _____   _____

Secret Key: ☐Start ☐End ☐Middle ☐Indicated Point ☐Split
Key Used: ☐ 1 ☐ 2 ☐ 3 ☐ 4 ☐ 5 ☐ 6 ☐ 7   _____

Account: _____ Additional Notes:

Username: _____ _____

Password: _____ _____

Secret Key: ☐Start ☐End ☐Middle ☐Indicated Point ☐Split
Key Used: ☐1 ☐2 ☐3 ☐4 ☐5 ☐6 ☐7 _____

Account: _____ Additional Notes:

Username: _____ _____

Password: _____ _____

Secret Key: ☐Start ☐End ☐Middle ☐Indicated Point ☐Split
Key Used: ☐1 ☐2 ☐3 ☐4 ☐5 ☐6 ☐7 _____

Account: _____ Additional Notes:

Username: _____ _____

Password: _____ _____

Secret Key: ☐Start ☐End ☐Middle ☐Indicated Point ☐Split
Key Used: ☐1 ☐2 ☐3 ☐4 ☐5 ☐6 ☐7 _____

Account: _____ Additional Notes:

Username: _____ _____

Password: _____ _____

Secret Key: ☐Start ☐End ☐Middle ☐Indicated Point ☐Split
Key Used: ☐1 ☐2 ☐3 ☐4 ☐5 ☐6 ☐7 _____

Account: _____ Additional Notes:

Username: _____ _____

Password: _____ _____

Secret Key: ☐Start ☐End ☐Middle ☐Indicated Point ☐Split
Key Used: ☐1 ☐2 ☐3 ☐4 ☐5 ☐6 ☐7 _____

The Encrypted Book of Passwords

Account: _____	Additional Notes:
Username: _____	_____
Password: _____	_____
Secret Key: ☐Start ☐End ☐Middle ☐Indicated Point ☐Split Key Used: ☐ 1 ☐ 2 ☐ 3 ☐ 4 ☐ 5 ☐ 6 ☐ 7	_____

Account: _____	Additional Notes:
Username: _____	_____
Password: _____	_____
Secret Key: ☐Start ☐End ☐Middle ☐Indicated Point ☐Split Key Used: ☐ 1 ☐ 2 ☐ 3 ☐ 4 ☐ 5 ☐ 6 ☐ 7	_____

Account: _____	Additional Notes:
Username: _____	_____
Password: _____	_____
Secret Key: ☐Start ☐End ☐Middle ☐Indicated Point ☐Split Key Used: ☐ 1 ☐ 2 ☐ 3 ☐ 4 ☐ 5 ☐ 6 ☐ 7	_____

Account: _____	Additional Notes:
Username: _____	_____
Password: _____	_____
Secret Key: ☐Start ☐End ☐Middle ☐Indicated Point ☐Split Key Used: ☐ 1 ☐ 2 ☐ 3 ☐ 4 ☐ 5 ☐ 6 ☐ 7	_____

Account: _____	Additional Notes:
Username: _____	_____
Password: _____	_____
Secret Key: ☐Start ☐End ☐Middle ☐Indicated Point ☐Split Key Used: ☐ 1 ☐ 2 ☐ 3 ☐ 4 ☐ 5 ☐ 6 ☐ 7	_____

I

Account: _____	Additional Notes:
Username: _____	_____
Password: _____	_____
Secret Key: ☐Start ☐End ☐Middle ☐Indicated Point ☐Split Key Used: ☐ 1 ☐ 2 ☐ 3 ☐ 4 ☐ 5 ☐ 6 ☐ 7	_____

Account: _____	Additional Notes:
Username: _____	_____
Password: _____	_____
Secret Key: ☐Start ☐End ☐Middle ☐Indicated Point ☐Split Key Used: ☐ 1 ☐ 2 ☐ 3 ☐ 4 ☐ 5 ☐ 6 ☐ 7	_____

Account: _____	Additional Notes:
Username: _____	_____
Password: _____	_____
Secret Key: ☐Start ☐End ☐Middle ☐Indicated Point ☐Split Key Used: ☐ 1 ☐ 2 ☐ 3 ☐ 4 ☐ 5 ☐ 6 ☐ 7	_____

Account: _____	Additional Notes:
Username: _____	_____
Password: _____	_____
Secret Key: ☐Start ☐End ☐Middle ☐Indicated Point ☐Split Key Used: ☐ 1 ☐ 2 ☐ 3 ☐ 4 ☐ 5 ☐ 6 ☐ 7	_____

Account: _____	Additional Notes:
Username: _____	_____
Password: _____	_____
Secret Key: ☐Start ☐End ☐Middle ☐Indicated Point ☐Split Key Used: ☐ 1 ☐ 2 ☐ 3 ☐ 4 ☐ 5 ☐ 6 ☐ 7	_____

Account: _____   Additional Notes:

Username: _____   _____

Password: _____   _____

Secret Key: ☐Start ☐End ☐Middle ☐Indicated Point ☐Split   _____
Key Used: ☐ 1 ☐ 2 ☐ 3 ☐ 4 ☐ 5 ☐ 6 ☐ 7

Account: _____   Additional Notes:

Username: _____   _____

Password: _____   _____

Secret Key: ☐Start ☐End ☐Middle ☐Indicated Point ☐Split   _____
Key Used: ☐ 1 ☐ 2 ☐ 3 ☐ 4 ☐ 5 ☐ 6 ☐ 7

Account: _____   Additional Notes:

Username: _____   _____

Password: _____   _____

Secret Key: ☐Start ☐End ☐Middle ☐Indicated Point ☐Split   _____
Key Used: ☐ 1 ☐ 2 ☐ 3 ☐ 4 ☐ 5 ☐ 6 ☐ 7

Account: _____   Additional Notes:

Username: _____   _____

Password: _____   _____

Secret Key: ☐Start ☐End ☐Middle ☐Indicated Point ☐Split   _____
Key Used: ☐ 1 ☐ 2 ☐ 3 ☐ 4 ☐ 5 ☐ 6 ☐ 7

Account: _____   Additional Notes:

Username: _____   _____

Password: _____   _____

Secret Key: ☐Start ☐End ☐Middle ☐Indicated Point ☐Split   _____
Key Used: ☐ 1 ☐ 2 ☐ 3 ☐ 4 ☐ 5 ☐ 6 ☐ 7

Account: _____ Additional Notes:

Username: _____ _____

Password: _____ _____

Secret Key: ☐Start ☐End ☐Middle ☐Indicated Point ☐Split _____
Key Used: ☐ 1 ☐ 2 ☐ 3 ☐ 4 ☐ 5 ☐ 6 ☐ 7

Account: _____ Additional Notes:

Username: _____ _____

Password: _____ _____

Secret Key: ☐Start ☐End ☐Middle ☐Indicated Point ☐Split _____
Key Used: ☐ 1 ☐ 2 ☐ 3 ☐ 4 ☐ 5 ☐ 6 ☐ 7

Account: _____ Additional Notes:

Username: _____ _____

Password: _____ _____

Secret Key: ☐Start ☐End ☐Middle ☐Indicated Point ☐Split _____
Key Used: ☐ 1 ☐ 2 ☐ 3 ☐ 4 ☐ 5 ☐ 6 ☐ 7

Account: _____ Additional Notes:

Username: _____ _____

Password: _____ _____

Secret Key: ☐Start ☐End ☐Middle ☐Indicated Point ☐Split _____
Key Used: ☐ 1 ☐ 2 ☐ 3 ☐ 4 ☐ 5 ☐ 6 ☐ 7

Account: _____ Additional Notes:

Username: _____ _____

Password: _____ _____

Secret Key: ☐Start ☐End ☐Middle ☐Indicated Point ☐Split _____
Key Used: ☐ 1 ☐ 2 ☐ 3 ☐ 4 ☐ 5 ☐ 6 ☐ 7

Account: _____   Additional Notes:

Username: _____

Password: _____   _____

Secret Key: ☐Start ☐End ☐Middle ☐Indicated Point ☐Split   _____
Key Used: ☐ 1 ☐ 2 ☐ 3 ☐ 4 ☐ 5 ☐ 6 ☐ 7

Account: _____   Additional Notes:

Username: _____

Password: _____   _____

Secret Key: ☐Start ☐End ☐Middle ☐Indicated Point ☐Split   _____
Key Used: ☐ 1 ☐ 2 ☐ 3 ☐ 4 ☐ 5 ☐ 6 ☐ 7

Account: _____   Additional Notes:

Username: _____

Password: _____   _____

Secret Key: ☐Start ☐End ☐Middle ☐Indicated Point ☐Split   _____
Key Used: ☐ 1 ☐ 2 ☐ 3 ☐ 4 ☐ 5 ☐ 6 ☐ 7

Account: _____   Additional Notes:

Username: _____

Password: _____   _____

Secret Key: ☐Start ☐End ☐Middle ☐Indicated Point ☐Split   _____
Key Used: ☐ 1 ☐ 2 ☐ 3 ☐ 4 ☐ 5 ☐ 6 ☐ 7

Account: _____   Additional Notes:

Username: _____

Password: _____   _____

Secret Key: ☐Start ☐End ☐Middle ☐Indicated Point ☐Split   _____
Key Used: ☐ 1 ☐ 2 ☐ 3 ☐ 4 ☐ 5 ☐ 6 ☐ 7

J

Account: _____	Additional Notes:
Username: _____	_____
Password: _____	_____
Secret Key: ☐Start ☐End ☐Middle ☐Indicated Point ☐Split Key Used: ☐1 ☐2 ☐3 ☐4 ☐5 ☐6 ☐7	_____

Account: _____	Additional Notes:
Username: _____	_____
Password: _____	_____
Secret Key: ☐Start ☐End ☐Middle ☐Indicated Point ☐Split Key Used: ☐1 ☐2 ☐3 ☐4 ☐5 ☐6 ☐7	_____

Account: _____	Additional Notes:
Username: _____	_____
Password: _____	_____
Secret Key: ☐Start ☐End ☐Middle ☐Indicated Point ☐Split Key Used: ☐1 ☐2 ☐3 ☐4 ☐5 ☐6 ☐7	_____

Account: _____	Additional Notes:
Username: _____	_____
Password: _____	_____
Secret Key: ☐Start ☐End ☐Middle ☐Indicated Point ☐Split Key Used: ☐1 ☐2 ☐3 ☐4 ☐5 ☐6 ☐7	_____

Account: _____	Additional Notes:
Username: _____	_____
Password: _____	_____
Secret Key: ☐Start ☐End ☐Middle ☐Indicated Point ☐Split Key Used: ☐1 ☐2 ☐3 ☐4 ☐5 ☐6 ☐7	_____

The Encrypted Book of Passwords

Account: _____   Additional Notes:

Username: _____   _____

Password: _____   _____

Secret Key: ☐Start ☐End ☐Middle ☐Indicated Point ☐Split   _____
Key Used: ☐ 1 ☐ 2 ☐ 3 ☐ 4 ☐ 5 ☐ 6 ☐ 7

Account: _____   Additional Notes:

Username: _____   _____

Password: _____   _____

Secret Key: ☐Start ☐End ☐Middle ☐Indicated Point ☐Split   _____
Key Used: ☐ 1 ☐ 2 ☐ 3 ☐ 4 ☐ 5 ☐ 6 ☐ 7

Account: _____   Additional Notes:

Username: _____   _____

Password: _____   _____

Secret Key: ☐Start ☐End ☐Middle ☐Indicated Point ☐Split   _____
Key Used: ☐ 1 ☐ 2 ☐ 3 ☐ 4 ☐ 5 ☐ 6 ☐ 7

Account: _____   Additional Notes:

Username: _____   _____

Password: _____   _____

Secret Key: ☐Start ☐End ☐Middle ☐Indicated Point ☐Split   _____
Key Used: ☐ 1 ☐ 2 ☐ 3 ☐ 4 ☐ 5 ☐ 6 ☐ 7

Account: _____   Additional Notes:

Username: _____   _____

Password: _____   _____

Secret Key: ☐Start ☐End ☐Middle ☐Indicated Point ☐Split   _____
Key Used: ☐ 1 ☐ 2 ☐ 3 ☐ 4 ☐ 5 ☐ 6 ☐ 7

Account: _____   Additional Notes:

Username: _____   _____

Password: _____   _____

Secret Key: ☐Start ☐End ☐Middle ☐Indicated Point ☐Split   _____
Key Used: ☐ 1 ☐ 2 ☐ 3 ☐ 4 ☐ 5 ☐ 6 ☐ 7

Account: _____   Additional Notes:

Username: _____   _____

Password: _____   _____

Secret Key: ☐Start ☐End ☐Middle ☐Indicated Point ☐Split   _____
Key Used: ☐ 1 ☐ 2 ☐ 3 ☐ 4 ☐ 5 ☐ 6 ☐ 7

Account: _____   Additional Notes:

Username: _____   _____

Password: _____   _____

Secret Key: ☐Start ☐End ☐Middle ☐Indicated Point ☐Split   _____
Key Used: ☐ 1 ☐ 2 ☐ 3 ☐ 4 ☐ 5 ☐ 6 ☐ 7

Account: _____   Additional Notes:

Username: _____   _____

Password: _____   _____

Secret Key: ☐Start ☐End ☐Middle ☐Indicated Point ☐Split   _____
Key Used: ☐ 1 ☐ 2 ☐ 3 ☐ 4 ☐ 5 ☐ 6 ☐ 7

Account: _____   Additional Notes:

Username: _____   _____

Password: _____   _____

Secret Key: ☐Start ☐End ☐Middle ☐Indicated Point ☐Split   _____
Key Used: ☐ 1 ☐ 2 ☐ 3 ☐ 4 ☐ 5 ☐ 6 ☐ 7

The Encrypted Book of Passwords

Account: _____	Additional Notes:
Username: _____	_____
Password: _____	_____
Secret Key: ☐Start ☐End ☐Middle ☐Indicated Point ☐Split	
Key Used: ☐1 ☐2 ☐3 ☐4 ☐5 ☐6 ☐7	_____

Account: _____	Additional Notes:
Username: _____	_____
Password: _____	_____
Secret Key: ☐Start ☐End ☐Middle ☐Indicated Point ☐Split	
Key Used: ☐1 ☐2 ☐3 ☐4 ☐5 ☐6 ☐7	_____

Account: _____	Additional Notes:
Username: _____	_____
Password: _____	_____
Secret Key: ☐Start ☐End ☐Middle ☐Indicated Point ☐Split	
Key Used: ☐1 ☐2 ☐3 ☐4 ☐5 ☐6 ☐7	_____

Account: _____	Additional Notes:
Username: _____	_____
Password: _____	_____
Secret Key: ☐Start ☐End ☐Middle ☐Indicated Point ☐Split	
Key Used: ☐1 ☐2 ☐3 ☐4 ☐5 ☐6 ☐7	_____

Account: _____	Additional Notes:
Username: _____	_____
Password: _____	_____
Secret Key: ☐Start ☐End ☐Middle ☐Indicated Point ☐Split	
Key Used: ☐1 ☐2 ☐3 ☐4 ☐5 ☐6 ☐7	_____

K

Account: _____	Additional Notes:
Username: _____	_____
Password: _____	_____
Secret Key: ☐Start ☐End ☐Middle ☐Indicated Point ☐Split	_____
Key Used: ☐ 1 ☐ 2 ☐ 3 ☐ 4 ☐ 5 ☐ 6 ☐ 7	

Account: _____	Additional Notes:
Username: _____	_____
Password: _____	_____
Secret Key: ☐Start ☐End ☐Middle ☐Indicated Point ☐Split	_____
Key Used: ☐ 1 ☐ 2 ☐ 3 ☐ 4 ☐ 5 ☐ 6 ☐ 7	

Account: _____	Additional Notes:
Username: _____	_____
Password: _____	_____
Secret Key: ☐Start ☐End ☐Middle ☐Indicated Point ☐Split	_____
Key Used: ☐ 1 ☐ 2 ☐ 3 ☐ 4 ☐ 5 ☐ 6 ☐ 7	

Account: _____	Additional Notes:
Username: _____	_____
Password: _____	_____
Secret Key: ☐Start ☐End ☐Middle ☐Indicated Point ☐Split	_____
Key Used: ☐ 1 ☐ 2 ☐ 3 ☐ 4 ☐ 5 ☐ 6 ☐ 7	

Account: _____	Additional Notes:
Username: _____	_____
Password: _____	_____
Secret Key: ☐Start ☐End ☐Middle ☐Indicated Point ☐Split	_____
Key Used: ☐ 1 ☐ 2 ☐ 3 ☐ 4 ☐ 5 ☐ 6 ☐ 7	

Account: _____   Additional Notes:

Username: _____   _____

Password: _____   _____

Secret Key: ☐Start ☐End ☐Middle ☐Indicated Point ☐Split   _____
Key Used: ☐ 1 ☐ 2 ☐ 3 ☐ 4 ☐ 5 ☐ 6 ☐ 7

Account: _____   Additional Notes:

Username: _____   _____

Password: _____   _____

Secret Key: ☐Start ☐End ☐Middle ☐Indicated Point ☐Split   _____
Key Used: ☐ 1 ☐ 2 ☐ 3 ☐ 4 ☐ 5 ☐ 6 ☐ 7

Account: _____   Additional Notes:

Username: _____   _____

Password: _____   _____

Secret Key: ☐Start ☐End ☐Middle ☐Indicated Point ☐Split   _____
Key Used: ☐ 1 ☐ 2 ☐ 3 ☐ 4 ☐ 5 ☐ 6 ☐ 7

Account: _____   Additional Notes:

Username: _____   _____

Password: _____   _____

Secret Key: ☐Start ☐End ☐Middle ☐Indicated Point ☐Split   _____
Key Used: ☐ 1 ☐ 2 ☐ 3 ☐ 4 ☐ 5 ☐ 6 ☐ 7

Account: _____   Additional Notes:

Username: _____   _____

Password: _____   _____

Secret Key: ☐Start ☐End ☐Middle ☐Indicated Point ☐Split   _____
Key Used: ☐ 1 ☐ 2 ☐ 3 ☐ 4 ☐ 5 ☐ 6 ☐ 7

Account: _____	Additional Notes:
Username: _____	_____
Password: _____	_____
Secret Key: ☐Start ☐End ☐Middle ☐Indicated Point ☐Split Key Used: ☐ 1 ☐ 2 ☐ 3 ☐ 4 ☐ 5 ☐ 6 ☐ 7	_____

Account: _____	Additional Notes:
Username: _____	_____
Password: _____	_____
Secret Key: ☐Start ☐End ☐Middle ☐Indicated Point ☐Split Key Used: ☐ 1 ☐ 2 ☐ 3 ☐ 4 ☐ 5 ☐ 6 ☐ 7	_____

Account: _____	Additional Notes:
Username: _____	_____
Password: _____	_____
Secret Key: ☐Start ☐End ☐Middle ☐Indicated Point ☐Split Key Used: ☐ 1 ☐ 2 ☐ 3 ☐ 4 ☐ 5 ☐ 6 ☐ 7	_____

Account: _____	Additional Notes:
Username: _____	_____
Password: _____	_____
Secret Key: ☐Start ☐End ☐Middle ☐Indicated Point ☐Split Key Used: ☐ 1 ☐ 2 ☐ 3 ☐ 4 ☐ 5 ☐ 6 ☐ 7	_____

Account: _____	Additional Notes.
Username: _____	_____
Password: _____	_____
Secret Key: ☐Start ☐End ☐Middle ☐Indicated Point ☐Split Key Used: ☐ 1 ☐ 2 ☐ 3 ☐ 4 ☐ 5 ☐ 6 ☐ 7	_____

The Encrypted Book of Passwords

Account: _____   Additional Notes:

Username: _____

Password: _____

Secret Key: ☐Start ☐End ☐Middle ☐Indicated Point ☐Split
Key Used: ☐ 1 ☐ 2 ☐ 3 ☐ 4 ☐ 5 ☐ 6 ☐ 7

Account: _____   Additional Notes:

Username: _____

Password: _____

Secret Key: ☐Start ☐End ☐Middle ☐Indicated Point ☐Split
Key Used: ☐ 1 ☐ 2 ☐ 3 ☐ 4 ☐ 5 ☐ 6 ☐ 7

Account: _____   Additional Notes:

Username: _____

Password: _____

Secret Key: ☐Start ☐End ☐Middle ☐Indicated Point ☐Split
Key Used: ☐ 1 ☐ 2 ☐ 3 ☐ 4 ☐ 5 ☐ 6 ☐ 7

Account: _____   Additional Notes:

Username: _____

Password: _____

Secret Key: ☐Start ☐End ☐Middle ☐Indicated Point ☐Split
Key Used: ☐ 1 ☐ 2 ☐ 3 ☐ 4 ☐ 5 ☐ 6 ☐ 7

Account: _____   Additional Notes:

Username: _____

Password: _____

Secret Key: ☐Start ☐End ☐Middle ☐Indicated Point ☐Split
Key Used: ☐ 1 ☐ 2 ☐ 3 ☐ 4 ☐ 5 ☐ 6 ☐ 7

L

Account: _____ Additional Notes:

Username: _____ _____

Password: _____ _____

Secret Key: ☐Start ☐End ☐Middle ☐Indicated Point ☐Split
Key Used: ☐1 ☐2 ☐3 ☐4 ☐5 ☐6 ☐7 _____

Account: _____ Additional Notes:

Username: _____ _____

Password: _____ _____

Secret Key: ☐Start ☐End ☐Middle ☐Indicated Point ☐Split
Key Used: ☐1 ☐2 ☐3 ☐4 ☐5 ☐6 ☐7 _____

Account: _____ Additional Notes:

Username: _____ _____

Password: _____ _____

Secret Key: ☐Start ☐End ☐Middle ☐Indicated Point ☐Split
Key Used: ☐1 ☐2 ☐3 ☐4 ☐5 ☐6 ☐7 _____

Account: _____ Additional Notes:

Username: _____ _____

Password: _____ _____

Secret Key: ☐Start ☐End ☐Middle ☐Indicated Point ☐Split
Key Used: ☐1 ☐2 ☐3 ☐4 ☐5 ☐6 ☐7 _____

Account: _____ Additional Notes:

Username: _____ _____

Password: _____ _____

Secret Key: ☐Start ☐End ☐Middle ☐Indicated Point ☐Split
Key Used: ☐1 ☐2 ☐3 ☐4 ☐5 ☐6 ☐7 _____

Account: _____	Additional Notes:
Username: _____	_____
Password: _____	_____
Secret Key: □Start □End □Middle □Indicated Point □Split Key Used: □ 1 □ 2 □ 3 □ 4 □ 5 □ 6 □ 7	_____

Account: _____	Additional Notes:
Username: _____	_____
Password: _____	_____
Secret Key: □Start □End □Middle □Indicated Point □Split Key Used: □ 1 □ 2 □ 3 □ 4 □ 5 □ 6 □ 7	_____

Account: _____	Additional Notes:
Username: _____	_____
Password: _____	_____
Secret Key: □Start □End □Middle □Indicated Point □Split Key Used: □ 1 □ 2 □ 3 □ 4 □ 5 □ 6 □ 7	_____

Account: _____	Additional Notes:
Username: _____	_____
Password: _____	_____
Secret Key: □Start □End □Middle □Indicated Point □Split Key Used: □ 1 □ 2 □ 3 □ 4 □ 5 □ 6 □ 7	_____

Account: _____	Additional Notes:
Username: _____	_____
Password: _____	_____
Secret Key: □Start □End □Middle □Indicated Point □Split Key Used: □ 1 □ 2 □ 3 □ 4 □ 5 □ 6 □ 7	_____

Account: _____	Additional Notes:
Username:	_____
Password: _____	_____
Secret Key: ☐Start ☐End ☐Middle ☐Indicated Point ☐Split Key Used: ☐ 1 ☐ 2 ☐ 3 ☐ 4 ☐ 5 ☐ 6 ☐ 7	_____

Account: _____	Additional Notes:
Username:	_____
Password: _____	_____
Secret Key: ☐Start ☐End ☐Middle ☐Indicated Point ☐Split Key Used: ☐ 1 ☐ 2 ☐ 3 ☐ 4 ☐ 5 ☐ 6 ☐ 7	_____

Account: _____	Additional Notes:
Username:	_____
Password: _____	_____
Secret Key: ☐Start ☐End ☐Middle ☐Indicated Point ☐Split Key Used: ☐ 1 ☐ 2 ☐ 3 ☐ 4 ☐ 5 ☐ 6 ☐ 7	_____

Account: _____	Additional Notes:
Username:	_____
Password: _____	_____
Secret Key: ☐Start ☐End ☐Middle ☐Indicated Point ☐Split Key Used: ☐ 1 ☐ 2 ☐ 3 ☐ 4 ☐ 5 ☐ 6 ☐ 7	_____

Account: _____	Additional Notes:
Username:	_____
Password: _____	_____
Secret Key: ☐Start ☐End ☐Middle ☐Indicated Point ☐Split Key Used: ☐ 1 ☐ 2 ☐ 3 ☐ 4 ☐ 5 ☐ 6 ☐ 7	_____

The Encrypted Book of Passwords

Account: _____	Additional Notes:
Username: _____	_____
Password: _____	_____
Secret Key: ☐Start ☐End ☐Middle ☐Indicated Point ☐Split Key Used: ☐1 ☐2 ☐3 ☐4 ☐5 ☐6 ☐7	_____

Account: _____	Additional Notes:
Username: _____	_____
Password: _____	_____
Secret Key: ☐Start ☐End ☐Middle ☐Indicated Point ☐Split Key Used: ☐1 ☐2 ☐3 ☐4 ☐5 ☐6 ☐7	_____

Account: _____	Additional Notes:
Username: _____	_____
Password: _____	_____
Secret Key: ☐Start ☐End ☐Middle ☐Indicated Point ☐Split Key Used: ☐1 ☐2 ☐3 ☐4 ☐5 ☐6 ☐7	_____

Account: _____	Additional Notes:
Username: _____	_____
Password: _____	_____
Secret Key: ☐Start ☐End ☐Middle ☐Indicated Point ☐Split Key Used: ☐1 ☐2 ☐3 ☐4 ☐5 ☐6 ☐7	_____

Account: _____	Additional Notes:
Username: _____	_____
Password: _____	_____
Secret Key: ☐Start ☐End ☐Middle ☐Indicated Point ☐Split Key Used: ☐1 ☐2 ☐3 ☐4 ☐5 ☐6 ☐7	_____

M

Account: _____ Additional Notes:

Username: _____ _____

Password: _____ _____

Secret Key: ☐Start ☐End ☐Middle ☐Indicated Point ☐Split
Key Used: ☐1 ☐2 ☐3 ☐4 ☐5 ☐6 ☐7 _____

Account: _____ Additional Notes:

Username: _____ _____

Password: _____ _____

Secret Key: ☐Start ☐End ☐Middle ☐Indicated Point ☐Split
Key Used: ☐1 ☐2 ☐3 ☐4 ☐5 ☐6 ☐7 _____

Account: _____ Additional Notes:

Username: _____ _____

Password: _____ _____

Secret Key: ☐Start ☐End ☐Middle ☐Indicated Point ☐Split
Key Used: ☐1 ☐2 ☐3 ☐4 ☐5 ☐6 ☐7 _____

Account: _____ Additional Notes:

Username: _____ _____

Password: _____ _____

Secret Key: ☐Start ☐End ☐Middle ☐Indicated Point ☐Split
Key Used: ☐1 ☐2 ☐3 ☐4 ☐5 ☐6 ☐7 _____

Account: _____ Additional Notes:

Username: _____ _____

Password: _____ _____

Secret Key: ☐Start ☐End ☐Middle ☐Indicated Point ☐Split
Key Used: ☐1 ☐2 ☐3 ☐4 ☐5 ☐6 ☐7 _____

Account: _____   Additional Notes:

Username: _____   _____

Password: _____   _____

Secret Key: ☐Start ☐End ☐Middle ☐Indicated Point ☐Split
Key Used: ☐ 1 ☐ 2 ☐ 3 ☐ 4 ☐ 5 ☐ 6 ☐ 7   _____

Account: _____   Additional Notes:

Username: _____   _____

Password: _____   _____

Secret Key: ☐Start ☐End ☐Middle ☐Indicated Point ☐Split
Key Used: ☐ 1 ☐ 2 ☐ 3 ☐ 4 ☐ 5 ☐ 6 ☐ 7   _____

Account: _____   Additional Notes:

Username: _____   _____

Password: _____   _____

Secret Key: ☐Start ☐End ☐Middle ☐Indicated Point ☐Split
Key Used: ☐ 1 ☐ 2 ☐ 3 ☐ 4 ☐ 5 ☐ 6 ☐ 7   _____

Account: _____   Additional Notes:

Username: _____   _____

Password: _____   _____

Secret Key: ☐Start ☐End ☐Middle ☐Indicated Point ☐Split
Key Used: ☐ 1 ☐ 2 ☐ 3 ☐ 4 ☐ 5 ☐ 6 ☐ 7   _____

Account: _____   Additional Notes:

Username: _____   _____

Password: _____   _____

Secret Key: ☐Start ☐End ☐Middle ☐Indicated Point ☐Split
Key Used: ☐ 1 ☐ 2 ☐ 3 ☐ 4 ☐ 5 ☐ 6 ☐ 7   _____

Account: _____   Additional Notes:

Username: _____   _____

Password: _____   _____

Secret Key: ☐Start ☐End ☐Middle ☐Indicated Point ☐Split   _____
Key Used: ☐ 1 ☐ 2 ☐ 3 ☐ 4 ☐ 5 ☐ 6 ☐ 7

Account: _____   Additional Notes:

Username: _____   _____

Password: _____   _____

Secret Key: ☐Start ☐End ☐Middle ☐Indicated Point ☐Split   _____
Key Used: ☐ 1 ☐ 2 ☐ 3 ☐ 4 ☐ 5 ☐ 6 ☐ 7

Account: _____   Additional Notes:

Username: _____   _____

Password: _____   _____

Secret Key: ☐Start ☐End ☐Middle ☐Indicated Point ☐Split   _____
Key Used: ☐ 1 ☐ 2 ☐ 3 ☐ 4 ☐ 5 ☐ 6 ☐ 7

Account: _____   Additional Notes:

Username: _____   _____

Password: _____   _____

Secret Key: ☐Start ☐End ☐Middle ☐Indicated Point ☐Split   _____
Key Used: ☐ 1 ☐ 2 ☐ 3 ☐ 4 ☐ 5 ☐ 6 ☐ 7

Account: _____   Additional Notes:

Username: _____   _____

Password: _____   _____

Secret Key: ☐Start ☐End ☐Middle ☐Indicated Point ☐Split   _____
Key Used: ☐ 1 ☐ 2 ☐ 3 ☐ 4 ☐ 5 ☐ 6 ☐ 7

The Encrypted Book of Passwords

Account: _____	Additional Notes:
Username: _____	_____
Password: _____	_____
Secret Key: ☐Start ☐End ☐Middle ☐Indicated Point ☐Split Key Used: ☐1 ☐2 ☐3 ☐4 ☐5 ☐6 ☐7	_____

Account: _____	Additional Notes:
Username: _____	_____
Password: _____	_____
Secret Key: ☐Start ☐End ☐Middle ☐Indicated Point ☐Split Key Used: ☐1 ☐2 ☐3 ☐4 ☐5 ☐6 ☐7	_____

Account: _____	Additional Notes:
Username: _____	_____
Password: _____	_____
Secret Key: ☐Start ☐End ☐Middle ☐Indicated Point ☐Split Key Used: ☐1 ☐2 ☐3 ☐4 ☐5 ☐6 ☐7	_____

Account: _____	Additional Notes:
Username: _____	_____
Password: _____	_____
Secret Key: ☐Start ☐End ☐Middle ☐Indicated Point ☐Split Key Used: ☐1 ☐2 ☐3 ☐4 ☐5 ☐6 ☐7	_____

Account: _____	Additional Notes:
Username: _____	_____
Password: _____	_____
Secret Key: ☐Start ☐End ☐Middle ☐Indicated Point ☐Split Key Used: ☐1 ☐2 ☐3 ☐4 ☐5 ☐6 ☐7	_____

N

Account: _____	Additional Notes:
Username: _____	_____
Password: _____	_____
Secret Key: ☐Start ☐End ☐Middle ☐Indicated Point ☐Split Key Used: ☐ 1 ☐ 2 ☐ 3 ☐ 4 ☐ 5 ☐ 6 ☐ 7	_____

Account: _____	Additional Notes:
Username: _____	_____
Password: _____	_____
Secret Key: ☐Start ☐End ☐Middle ☐Indicated Point ☐Split Key Used: ☐ 1 ☐ 2 ☐ 3 ☐ 4 ☐ 5 ☐ 6 ☐ 7	_____

Account: _____	Additional Notes:
Username: _____	_____
Password: _____	_____
Secret Key: ☐Start ☐End ☐Middle ☐Indicated Point ☐Split Key Used: ☐ 1 ☐ 2 ☐ 3 ☐ 4 ☐ 5 ☐ 6 ☐ 7	_____

Account: _____	Additional Notes:
Username: _____	_____
Password: _____	_____
Secret Key: ☐Start ☐End ☐Middle ☐Indicated Point ☐Split Key Used: ☐ 1 ☐ 2 ☐ 3 ☐ 4 ☐ 5 ☐ 6 ☐ 7	_____

Account: _____	Additional Notes:
Username: _____	_____
Password: _____	_____
Secret Key: ☐Start ☐End ☐Middle ☐Indicated Point ☐Split Key Used: ☐ 1 ☐ 2 ☐ 3 ☐ 4 ☐ 5 ☐ 6 ☐ 7	_____

Account: _____   Additional Notes:

Username: _____   _____

Password: _____   _____

Secret Key: ☐Start ☐End ☐Middle ☐Indicated Point ☐Split
Key Used: ☐ 1 ☐ 2 ☐ 3 ☐ 4 ☐ 5 ☐ 6 ☐ 7   _____

Account: _____   Additional Notes:

Username: _____   _____

Password: _____   _____

Secret Key: ☐Start ☐End ☐Middle ☐Indicated Point ☐Split
Key Used: ☐ 1 ☐ 2 ☐ 3 ☐ 4 ☐ 5 ☐ 6 ☐ 7   _____

Account: _____   Additional Notes:

Username: _____   _____

Password: _____   _____

Secret Key: ☐Start ☐End ☐Middle ☐Indicated Point ☐Split
Key Used: ☐ 1 ☐ 2 ☐ 3 ☐ 4 ☐ 5 ☐ 6 ☐ 7   _____

Account: _____   Additional Notes:

Username: _____   _____

Password: _____   _____

Secret Key: ☐Start ☐End ☐Middle ☐Indicated Point ☐Split
Key Used: ☐ 1 ☐ 2 ☐ 3 ☐ 4 ☐ 5 ☐ 6 ☐ 7   _____

Account: _____   Additional Notes:

Username: _____   _____

Password: _____   _____

Secret Key: ☐Start ☐End ☐Middle ☐Indicated Point ☐Split
Key Used: ☐ 1 ☐ 2 ☐ 3 ☐ 4 ☐ 5 ☐ 6 ☐ 7   _____

Account: _____   Additional Notes:

Username: _____   _____

Password: _____   _____

Secret Key: ☐Start ☐End ☐Middle ☐Indicated Point ☐Split
Key Used: ☐ 1 ☐ 2 ☐ 3 ☐ 4 ☐ 5 ☐ 6 ☐ 7   _____

Account: _____   Additional Notes:

Username: _____   _____

Password: _____   _____

Secret Key: ☐Start ☐End ☐Middle ☐Indicated Point ☐Split
Key Used: ☐ 1 ☐ 2 ☐ 3 ☐ 4 ☐ 5 ☐ 6 ☐ 7   _____

Account: _____   Additional Notes:

Username: _____   _____

Password: _____   _____

Secret Key: ☐Start ☐End ☐Middle ☐Indicated Point ☐Split
Key Used: ☐ 1 ☐ 2 ☐ 3 ☐ 4 ☐ 5 ☐ 6 ☐ 7   _____

Account: _____   Additional Notes:

Username: _____   _____

Password: _____   _____

Secret Key: ☐Start ☐End ☐Middle ☐Indicated Point ☐Split
Key Used: ☐ 1 ☐ 2 ☐ 3 ☐ 4 ☐ 5 ☐ 6 ☐ 7   _____

Account: _____   Additional Notes:

Username: _____   _____

Password: _____   _____

Secret Key: ☐Start ☐End ☐Middle ☐Indicated Point ☐Split
Key Used: ☐ 1 ☐ 2 ☐ 3 ☐ 4 ☐ 5 ☐ 6 ☐ 7   _____

The Encrypted Book of Passwords

Account: _____	Additional Notes:
Username: _____	_____
Password: _____	_____
Secret Key: ☐Start ☐End ☐Middle ☐Indicated Point ☐Split	_____
Key Used: ☐ 1 ☐ 2 ☐ 3 ☐ 4 ☐ 5 ☐ 6 ☐ 7	

Account: _____	Additional Notes:
Username: _____	_____
Password: _____	_____
Secret Key: ☐Start ☐End ☐Middle ☐Indicated Point ☐Split	_____
Key Used: ☐ 1 ☐ 2 ☐ 3 ☐ 4 ☐ 5 ☐ 6 ☐ 7	

Account: _____	Additional Notes:
Username: _____	_____
Password: _____	_____
Secret Key: ☐Start ☐End ☐Middle ☐Indicated Point ☐Split	_____
Key Used: ☐ 1 ☐ 2 ☐ 3 ☐ 4 ☐ 5 ☐ 6 ☐ 7	

Account: _____	Additional Notes:
Username: _____	_____
Password: _____	_____
Secret Key: ☐Start ☐End ☐Middle ☐Indicated Point ☐Split	_____
Key Used: ☐ 1 ☐ 2 ☐ 3 ☐ 4 ☐ 5 ☐ 6 ☐ 7	

Account: _____	Additional Notes:
Username: _____	_____
Password: _____	_____
Secret Key: ☐Start ☐End ☐Middle ☐Indicated Point ☐Split	_____
Key Used: ☐ 1 ☐ 2 ☐ 3 ☐ 4 ☐ 5 ☐ 6 ☐ 7	

O

Account: _____	Additional Notes:
Username: _____	_____
Password: _____	_____
Secret Key: □Start □End □Middle □Indicated Point □Split Key Used: □ 1 □ 2 □ 3 □ 4 □ 5 □ 6 □ 7	_____

Account: _____	Additional Notes:
Username: _____	_____
Password: _____	_____
Secret Key: □Start □End □Middle □Indicated Point □Split Key Used: □ 1 □ 2 □ 3 □ 4 □ 5 □ 6 □ 7	_____

Account: _____	Additional Notes:
Username: _____	_____
Password: _____	_____
Secret Key: □Start □End □Middle □Indicated Point □Split Key Used: □ 1 □ 2 □ 3 □ 4 □ 5 □ 6 □ 7	_____

Account: _____	Additional Notes:
Username: _____	_____
Password: _____	_____
Secret Key: □Start □End □Middle □Indicated Point □Split Key Used: □ 1 □ 2 □ 3 □ 4 □ 5 □ 6 □ 7	_____

Account: _____	Additional Notes:
Username: _____	_____
Password: _____	_____
Secret Key: □Start □End □Middle □Indicated Point □Split Key Used: □ 1 □ 2 □ 3 □ 4 □ 5 □ 6 □ 7	_____

The Encrypted Book of Passwords

Account: _____	Additional Notes:
Username: _____	_____
Password: _____	_____
Secret Key: ☐Start ☐End ☐Middle ☐Indicated Point ☐Split	_____
Key Used: ☐ 1 ☐ 2 ☐ 3 ☐ 4 ☐ 5 ☐ 6 ☐ 7	

Account: _____	Additional Notes:
Username: _____	_____
Password: _____	_____
Secret Key: ☐Start ☐End ☐Middle ☐Indicated Point ☐Split	_____
Key Used: ☐ 1 ☐ 2 ☐ 3 ☐ 4 ☐ 5 ☐ 6 ☐ 7	

Account: _____	Additional Notes:
Username: _____	_____
Password: _____	_____
Secret Key: ☐Start ☐End ☐Middle ☐Indicated Point ☐Split	_____
Key Used: ☐ 1 ☐ 2 ☐ 3 ☐ 4 ☐ 5 ☐ 6 ☐ 7	

Account: _____	Additional Notes:
Username: _____	_____
Password: _____	_____
Secret Key: ☐Start ☐End ☐Middle ☐Indicated Point ☐Split	_____
Key Used: ☐ 1 ☐ 2 ☐ 3 ☐ 4 ☐ 5 ☐ 6 ☐ 7	

Account: _____	Additional Notes:
Username: _____	_____
Password: _____	_____
Secret Key: ☐Start ☐End ☐Middle ☐Indicated Point ☐Split	_____
Key Used: ☐ 1 ☐ 2 ☐ 3 ☐ 4 ☐ 5 ☐ 6 ☐ 7	

Account: _____	Additional Notes:
Username: _____	_____
Password: _____	_____
Secret Key: ☐Start ☐End ☐Middle ☐Indicated Point ☐Split	_____
Key Used: ☐1 ☐2 ☐3 ☐4 ☐5 ☐6 ☐7	

Account: _____	Additional Notes:
Username: _____	_____
Password: _____	_____
Secret Key: ☐Start ☐End ☐Middle ☐Indicated Point ☐Split	_____
Key Used: ☐1 ☐2 ☐3 ☐4 ☐5 ☐6 ☐7	

Account: _____	Additional Notes:
Username: _____	_____
Password: _____	_____
Secret Key: ☐Start ☐End ☐Middle ☐Indicated Point ☐Split	_____
Key Used: ☐1 ☐2 ☐3 ☐4 ☐5 ☐6 ☐7	

Account: _____	Additional Notes:
Username: _____	_____
Password: _____	_____
Secret Key: ☐Start ☐End ☐Middle ☐Indicated Point ☐Split	_____
Key Used: ☐1 ☐2 ☐3 ☐4 ☐5 ☐6 ☐7	

Account: _____	Additional Notes:
Username: _____	_____
Password: _____	_____
Secret Key: ☐Start ☐End ☐Middle ☐Indicated Point ☐Split	_____
Key Used: ☐1 ☐2 ☐3 ☐4 ☐5 ☐6 ☐7	

Account: _____   Additional Notes:

Username: _____

Password: _____   _____

Secret Key: □Start □End □Middle □Indicated Point □Split
Key Used: □ 1 □ 2 □ 3 □ 4 □ 5 □ 6 □ 7   _____

Account: _____   Additional Notes:

Username: _____

Password: _____   _____

Secret Key: □Start □End □Middle □Indicated Point □Split
Key Used: □ 1 □ 2 □ 3 □ 4 □ 5 □ 6 □ 7   _____

Account: _____   Additional Notes:

Username: _____

Password: _____   _____

Secret Key: □Start □End □Middle □Indicated Point □Split
Key Used: □ 1 □ 2 □ 3 □ 4 □ 5 □ 6 □ 7   _____

Account: _____   Additional Notes:

Username: _____

Password: _____   _____

Secret Key: □Start □End □Middle □Indicated Point □Split
Key Used: □ 1 □ 2 □ 3 □ 4 □ 5 □ 6 □ 7   _____

Account: _____   Additional Notes:

Username: _____

Password: _____   _____

Secret Key: □Start □End □Middle □Indicated Point □Split
Key Used: □ 1 □ 2 □ 3 □ 4 □ 5 □ 6 □ 7   _____

P

Account: _____	Additional Notes:
Username: _____	_____
Password: _____	_____
Secret Key: ☐Start ☐End ☐Middle ☐Indicated Point ☐Split Key Used: ☐1 ☐2 ☐3 ☐4 ☐5 ☐6 ☐7	_____

Account: _____	Additional Notes:
Username: _____	_____
Password: _____	_____
Secret Key: ☐Start ☐End ☐Middle ☐Indicated Point ☐Split Key Used: ☐1 ☐2 ☐3 ☐4 ☐5 ☐6 ☐7	_____

Account: _____	Additional Notes:
Username: _____	_____
Password: _____	_____
Secret Key: ☐Start ☐End ☐Middle ☐Indicated Point ☐Split Key Used: ☐1 ☐2 ☐3 ☐4 ☐5 ☐6 ☐7	_____

Account: _____	Additional Notes:
Username: _____	_____
Password: _____	_____
Secret Key: ☐Start ☐End ☐Middle ☐Indicated Point ☐Split Key Used: ☐1 ☐2 ☐3 ☐4 ☐5 ☐6 ☐7	_____

Account: _____	Additional Notes:
Username: _____	_____
Password: _____	_____
Secret Key: ☐Start ☐End ☐Middle ☐Indicated Point ☐Split Key Used: ☐1 ☐2 ☐3 ☐4 ☐5 ☐6 ☐7	_____

The Encrypted Book of Passwords

Account: _____	Additional Notes:
Username: _____	_____
Password: _____	_____
Secret Key: ☐Start ☐End ☐Middle ☐Indicated Point ☐Split Key Used: ☐ 1 ☐ 2 ☐ 3 ☐ 4 ☐ 5☐ 6 ☐ 7	_____

Account: _____	Additional Notes:
Username: _____	_____
Password: _____	_____
Secret Key: ☐Start ☐End ☐Middle ☐Indicated Point ☐Split Key Used: ☐ 1 ☐ 2 ☐ 3 ☐ 4 ☐ 5☐ 6 ☐ 7	_____

Account: _____	Additional Notes:
Username: _____	_____
Password: _____	_____
Secret Key: ☐Start ☐End ☐Middle ☐Indicated Point ☐Split Key Used: ☐ 1 ☐ 2 ☐ 3 ☐ 4 ☐ 5☐ 6 ☐ 7	_____

Account: _____	Additional Notes:
Username: _____	_____
Password: _____	_____
Secret Key: ☐Start ☐End ☐Middle ☐Indicated Point ☐Split Key Used: ☐ 1 ☐ 2 ☐ 3 ☐ 4 ☐ 5☐ 6 ☐ 7	_____

Account: _____	Additional Notes:
Username: _____	_____
Password: _____	_____
Secret Key: ☐Start ☐End ☐Middle ☐Indicated Point ☐Split Key Used: ☐ 1 ☐ 2 ☐ 3 ☐ 4 ☐ 5☐ 6 ☐ 7	_____

Account: _____ Additional Notes:

Username: _____ _____

Password: _____ _____

Secret Key: ☐Start ☐End ☐Middle ☐Indicated Point ☐Split
Key Used: ☐ 1 ☐ 2 ☐ 3 ☐ 4 ☐ 5 ☐ 6 ☐ 7 _____

Account: _____ Additional Notes:

Username: _____ _____

Password: _____ _____

Secret Key: ☐Start ☐End ☐Middle ☐Indicated Point ☐Split
Key Used: ☐ 1 ☐ 2 ☐ 3 ☐ 4 ☐ 5 ☐ 6 ☐ 7 _____

Account: _____ Additional Notes:

Username: _____ _____

Password: _____ _____

Secret Key: ☐Start ☐End ☐Middle ☐Indicated Point ☐Split
Key Used: ☐ 1 ☐ 2 ☐ 3 ☐ 4 ☐ 5 ☐ 6 ☐ 7 _____

Account: _____ Additional Notes:

Username: _____ _____

Password: _____ _____

Secret Key: ☐Start ☐End ☐Middle ☐Indicated Point ☐Split
Key Used: ☐ 1 ☐ 2 ☐ 3 ☐ 4 ☐ 5 ☐ 6 ☐ 7 _____

Account: _____ Additional Notes:

Username: _____ _____

Password: _____ _____

Secret Key: ☐Start ☐End ☐Middle ☐Indicated Point ☐Split
Key Used: ☐ 1 ☐ 2 ☐ 3 ☐ 4 ☐ 5 ☐ 6 ☐ 7 _____

Account: _____   Additional Notes:

Username: _____   _____

Password: _____   _____

Secret Key: ☐Start ☐End ☐Middle ☐Indicated Point ☐Split   _____
Key Used: ☐ 1 ☐ 2 ☐ 3 ☐ 4 ☐ 5 ☐ 6 ☐ 7

Account: _____   Additional Notes:

Username: _____   _____

Password: _____   _____

Secret Key: ☐Start ☐End ☐Middle ☐Indicated Point ☐Split   _____
Key Used: ☐ 1 ☐ 2 ☐ 3 ☐ 4 ☐ 5 ☐ 6 ☐ 7

Account: _____   Additional Notes:

Username: _____   _____

Password: _____   _____

Secret Key: ☐Start ☐End ☐Middle ☐Indicated Point ☐Split   _____
Key Used: ☐ 1 ☐ 2 ☐ 3 ☐ 4 ☐ 5 ☐ 6 ☐ 7

Account: _____   Additional Notes:

Username: _____   _____

Password: _____   _____

Secret Key: ☐Start ☐End ☐Middle ☐Indicated Point ☐Split   _____
Key Used: ☐ 1 ☐ 2 ☐ 3 ☐ 4 ☐ 5 ☐ 6 ☐ 7

Account: _____   Additional Notes:

Username: _____   _____

Password: _____   _____

Secret Key: ☐Start ☐End ☐Middle ☐Indicated Point ☐Split   _____
Key Used: ☐ 1 ☐ 2 ☐ 3 ☐ 4 ☐ 5 ☐ 6 ☐ 7

Q

Entry 1
Account: _____
Username: _____
Password: _____
Secret Key: ☐Start ☐End ☐Middle ☐Indicated Point ☐Split
Key Used: ☐1 ☐2 ☐3 ☐4 ☐5 ☐6 ☐7
Additional Notes: _____

Entry 2
Account: _____
Username: _____
Password: _____
Secret Key: ☐Start ☐End ☐Middle ☐Indicated Point ☐Split
Key Used: ☐1 ☐2 ☐3 ☐4 ☐5 ☐6 ☐7
Additional Notes: _____

Entry 3
Account: _____
Username: _____
Password: _____
Secret Key: ☐Start ☐End ☐Middle ☐Indicated Point ☐Split
Key Used: ☐1 ☐2 ☐3 ☐4 ☐5 ☐6 ☐7
Additional Notes: _____

Entry 4
Account: _____
Username: _____
Password: _____
Secret Key: ☐Start ☐End ☐Middle ☐Indicated Point ☐Split
Key Used: ☐1 ☐2 ☐3 ☐4 ☐5 ☐6 ☐7
Additional Notes: _____

Entry 5
Account: _____
Username: _____
Password: _____
Secret Key: ☐Start ☐End ☐Middle ☐Indicated Point ☐Split
Key Used: ☐1 ☐2 ☐3 ☐4 ☐5 ☐6 ☐7
Additional Notes: _____

The Encrypted Book of Passwords

Account: _____   Additional Notes:

Username: _____   _____

Password: _____   _____

Secret Key: ☐Start ☐End ☐Middle ☐Indicated Point ☐Split   _____
Key Used: ☐ 1 ☐ 2 ☐ 3 ☐ 4 ☐ 5 ☐ 6 ☐ 7

Account: _____   Additional Notes:

Username: _____   _____

Password: _____   _____

Secret Key: ☐Start ☐End ☐Middle ☐Indicated Point ☐Split   _____
Key Used: ☐ 1 ☐ 2 ☐ 3 ☐ 4 ☐ 5 ☐ 6 ☐ 7

Account: _____   Additional Notes:

Username: _____   _____

Password: _____   _____

Secret Key: ☐Start ☐End ☐Middle ☐Indicated Point ☐Split   _____
Key Used: ☐ 1 ☐ 2 ☐ 3 ☐ 4 ☐ 5 ☐ 6 ☐ 7

Account: _____   Additional Notes:

Username: _____   _____

Password: _____   _____

Secret Key: ☐Start ☐End ☐Middle ☐Indicated Point ☐Split   _____
Key Used: ☐ 1 ☐ 2 ☐ 3 ☐ 4 ☐ 5 ☐ 6 ☐ 7

Account: _____   Additional Notes:

Username: _____   _____

Password: _____   _____

Secret Key: ☐Start ☐End ☐Middle ☐Indicated Point ☐Split   _____
Key Used: ☐ 1 ☐ 2 ☐ 3 ☐ 4 ☐ 5 ☐ 6 ☐ 7

R

Account: _____   Additional Notes:

Username: _____   _____

Password: _____   _____

Secret Key: ☐Start ☐End ☐Middle ☐Indicated Point ☐Split
Key Used: ☐ 1 ☐ 2 ☐ 3 ☐ 4 ☐ 5 ☐ 6 ☐ 7   _____

Account: _____   Additional Notes:

Username: _____   _____

Password: _____   _____

Secret Key: ☐Start ☐End ☐Middle ☐Indicated Point ☐Split
Key Used: ☐ 1 ☐ 2 ☐ 3 ☐ 4 ☐ 5 ☐ 6 ☐ 7   _____

Account: _____   Additional Notes:

Username: _____   _____

Password: _____   _____

Secret Key: ☐Start ☐End ☐Middle ☐Indicated Point ☐Split
Key Used: ☐ 1 ☐ 2 ☐ 3 ☐ 4 ☐ 5 ☐ 6 ☐ 7   _____

Account: _____   Additional Notes:

Username: _____   _____

Password: _____   _____

Secret Key: ☐Start ☐End ☐Middle ☐Indicated Point ☐Split
Key Used: ☐ 1 ☐ 2 ☐ 3 ☐ 4 ☐ 5 ☐ 6 ☐ 7   _____

Account: _____   Additional Notes:

Username: _____   _____

Password: _____   _____

Secret Key: ☐Start ☐End ☐Middle ☐Indicated Point ☐Split
Key Used: ☐ 1 ☐ 2 ☐ 3 ☐ 4 ☐ 5 ☐ 6 ☐ 7   _____

The Encrypted Book of Passwords

Account: _____	Additional Notes:
Username: _____	_____
Password: _____	_____
Secret Key: ☐Start ☐End ☐Middle ☐Indicated Point ☐Split Key Used: ☐ 1 ☐ 2 ☐ 3 ☐ 4 ☐ 5 ☐ 6 ☐ 7	_____

Account: _____	Additional Notes:
Username: _____	_____
Password: _____	_____
Secret Key: ☐Start ☐End ☐Middle ☐Indicated Point ☐Split Key Used: ☐ 1 ☐ 2 ☐ 3 ☐ 4 ☐ 5 ☐ 6 ☐ 7	_____

Account: _____	Additional Notes:
Username: _____	_____
Password: _____	_____
Secret Key: ☐Start ☐End ☐Middle ☐Indicated Point ☐Split Key Used: ☐ 1 ☐ 2 ☐ 3 ☐ 4 ☐ 5 ☐ 6 ☐ 7	_____

Account: _____	Additional Notes:
Username: _____	_____
Password: _____	_____
Secret Key: ☐Start ☐End ☐Middle ☐Indicated Point ☐Split Key Used: ☐ 1 ☐ 2 ☐ 3 ☐ 4 ☐ 5 ☐ 6 ☐ 7	_____

Account: _____	Additional Notes:
Username: _____	_____
Password: _____	_____
Secret Key: ☐Start ☐End ☐Middle ☐Indicated Point ☐Split Key Used: ☐ 1 ☐ 2 ☐ 3 ☐ 4 ☐ 5 ☐ 6 ☐ 7	_____

Account: _____   Additional Notes:

Username: _____   _____

Password: _____   _____

Secret Key: ☐Start ☐End ☐Middle ☐Indicated Point ☐Split
Key Used: ☐ 1 ☐ 2 ☐ 3 ☐ 4 ☐ 5 ☐ 6 ☐ 7   _____

Account: _____   Additional Notes:

Username: _____   _____

Password: _____   _____

Secret Key: ☐Start ☐End ☐Middle ☐Indicated Point ☐Split
Key Used: ☐ 1 ☐ 2 ☐ 3 ☐ 4 ☐ 5 ☐ 6 ☐ 7   _____

Account: _____   Additional Notes:

Username: _____   _____

Password: _____   _____

Secret Key: ☐Start ☐End ☐Middle ☐Indicated Point ☐Split
Key Used: ☐ 1 ☐ 2 ☐ 3 ☐ 4 ☐ 5 ☐ 6 ☐ 7   _____

Account: _____   Additional Notes:

Username: _____   _____

Password: _____   _____

Secret Key: ☐Start ☐End ☐Middle ☐Indicated Point ☐Split
Key Used: ☐ 1 ☐ 2 ☐ 3 ☐ 4 ☐ 5 ☐ 6 ☐ 7   _____

Account: _____   Additional Notes:

Username: _____   _____

Password: _____   _____

Secret Key: ☐Start ☐End ☐Middle ☐Indicated Point ☐Split
Key Used: ☐ 1 ☐ 2 ☐ 3 ☐ 4 ☐ 5 ☐ 6 ☐ 7   _____

Account: _____   Additional Notes:

Username: _____   _____

Password: _____   _____

Secret Key: ☐Start ☐End ☐Middle ☐Indicated Point ☐Split   _____
Key Used: ☐ 1 ☐ 2 ☐ 3 ☐ 4 ☐ 5 ☐ 6 ☐ 7

Account: _____   Additional Notes:

Username: _____   _____

Password: _____   _____

Secret Key: ☐Start ☐End ☐Middle ☐Indicated Point ☐Split   _____
Key Used: ☐ 1 ☐ 2 ☐ 3 ☐ 4 ☐ 5 ☐ 6 ☐ 7

Account: _____   Additional Notes:

Username: _____   _____

Password: _____   _____

Secret Key: ☐Start ☐End ☐Middle ☐Indicated Point ☐Split   _____
Key Used: ☐ 1 ☐ 2 ☐ 3 ☐ 4 ☐ 5 ☐ 6 ☐ 7

Account: _____   Additional Notes:

Username: _____   _____

Password: _____   _____

Secret Key: ☐Start ☐End ☐Middle ☐Indicated Point ☐Split   _____
Key Used: ☐ 1 ☐ 2 ☐ 3 ☐ 4 ☐ 5 ☐ 6 ☐ 7

Account: _____   Additional Notes:

Username: _____   _____

Password: _____   _____

Secret Key: ☐Start ☐End ☐Middle ☐Indicated Point ☐Split   _____
Key Used: ☐ 1 ☐ 2 ☐ 3 ☐ 4 ☐ 5 ☐ 6 ☐ 7

S

Account:	Additional Notes:
Username:	
Password:	
Secret Key: ☐Start ☐End ☐Middle ☐Indicated Point ☐Split	
Key Used: ☐ 1 ☐ 2 ☐ 3 ☐ 4 ☐ 5 ☐ 6 ☐ 7	

Account:	Additional Notes:
Username:	
Password:	
Secret Key: ☐Start ☐End ☐Middle ☐Indicated Point ☐Split	
Key Used: ☐ 1 ☐ 2 ☐ 3 ☐ 4 ☐ 5 ☐ 6 ☐ 7	

Account:	Additional Notes:
Username:	
Password:	
Secret Key: ☐Start ☐End ☐Middle ☐Indicated Point ☐Split	
Key Used: ☐ 1 ☐ 2 ☐ 3 ☐ 4 ☐ 5 ☐ 6 ☐ 7	

Account:	Additional Notes:
Username:	
Password:	
Secret Key: ☐Start ☐End ☐Middle ☐Indicated Point ☐Split	
Key Used: ☐ 1 ☐ 2 ☐ 3 ☐ 4 ☐ 5 ☐ 6 ☐ 7	

Account:	Additional Notes:
Username:	
Password:	
Secret Key: ☐Start ☐End ☐Middle ☐Indicated Point ☐Split	
Key Used: ☐ 1 ☐ 2 ☐ 3 ☐ 4 ☐ 5 ☐ 6 ☐ 7	

Account: _____   Additional Notes:

Username: _____   _____

Password: _____   _____

Secret Key: ☐Start ☐End ☐Middle ☐Indicated Point ☐Split   _____
Key Used: ☐ 1 ☐ 2 ☐ 3 ☐ 4 ☐ 5 ☐ 6 ☐ 7

Account: _____   Additional Notes:

Username: _____   _____

Password: _____   _____

Secret Key: ☐Start ☐End ☐Middle ☐Indicated Point ☐Split   _____
Key Used: ☐ 1 ☐ 2 ☐ 3 ☐ 4 ☐ 5 ☐ 6 ☐ 7

Account: _____   Additional Notes:

Username: _____   _____

Password: _____   _____

Secret Key: ☐Start ☐End ☐Middle ☐Indicated Point ☐Split   _____
Key Used: ☐ 1 ☐ 2 ☐ 3 ☐ 4 ☐ 5 ☐ 6 ☐ 7

Account: _____   Additional Notes:

Username: _____   _____

Password: _____   _____

Secret Key: ☐Start ☐End ☐Middle ☐Indicated Point ☐Split   _____
Key Used: ☐ 1 ☐ 2 ☐ 3 ☐ 4 ☐ 5 ☐ 6 ☐ 7

Account: _____   Additional Notes:

Username: _____   _____

Password: _____   _____

Secret Key: ☐Start ☐End ☐Middle ☐Indicated Point ☐Split   _____
Key Used: ☐ 1 ☐ 2 ☐ 3 ☐ 4 ☐ 5 ☐ 6 ☐ 7

Account: _____ Additional Notes:

Username: _____ _____

Password: _____ _____

Secret Key: □Start □End □Middle □Indicated Point □Split _____
Key Used: □ 1 □ 2 □ 3 □ 4 □ 5 □ 6 □ 7

Account: _____ Additional Notes:

Username: _____ _____

Password: _____ _____

Secret Key: □Start □End □Middle □Indicated Point □Split _____
Key Used: □ 1 □ 2 □ 3 □ 4 □ 5 □ 6 □ 7

Account: _____ Additional Notes:

Username: _____ _____

Password: _____ _____

Secret Key: □Start □End □Middle □Indicated Point □Split _____
Key Used: □ 1 □ 2 □ 3 □ 4 □ 5 □ 6 □ 7

Account: _____ Additional Notes:

Username: _____ _____

Password: _____ _____

Secret Key: □Start □End □Middle □Indicated Point □Split _____
Key Used: □ 1 □ 2 □ 3 □ 4 □ 5 □ 6 □ 7

Account: _____ Additional Notes:

Username: _____ _____

Password: _____ _____

Secret Key: □Start □End □Middle □Indicated Point □Split _____
Key Used: □ 1 □ 2 □ 3 □ 4 □ 5 □ 6 □ 7

Account: _____   Additional Notes:

Username: _____   _____

Password: _____   _____

Secret Key: ☐Start ☐End ☐Middle ☐Indicated Point ☐Split
Key Used: ☐ 1 ☐ 2 ☐ 3 ☐ 4 ☐ 5 ☐ 6 ☐ 7   _____

Account: _____   Additional Notes:

Username: _____   _____

Password: _____   _____

Secret Key: ☐Start ☐End ☐Middle ☐Indicated Point ☐Split
Key Used: ☐ 1 ☐ 2 ☐ 3 ☐ 4 ☐ 5 ☐ 6 ☐ 7   _____

Account: _____   Additional Notes:

Username: _____   _____

Password: _____   _____

Secret Key: ☐Start ☐End ☐Middle ☐Indicated Point ☐Split
Key Used: ☐ 1 ☐ 2 ☐ 3 ☐ 4 ☐ 5 ☐ 6 ☐ 7   _____

Account: _____   Additional Notes:

Username: _____   _____

Password: _____   _____

Secret Key: ☐Start ☐End ☐Middle ☐Indicated Point ☐Split
Key Used: ☐ 1 ☐ 2 ☐ 3 ☐ 4 ☐ 5 ☐ 6 ☐ 7   _____

Account: _____   Additional Notes:

Username: _____   _____

Password: _____   _____

Secret Key: ☐Start ☐End ☐Middle ☐Indicated Point ☐Split
Key Used: ☐ 1 ☐ 2 ☐ 3 ☐ 4 ☐ 5 ☐ 6 ☐ 7   _____

T

Account: _____	Additional Notes:
Username:	_____
Password:	_____
Secret Key: ☐Start ☐End ☐Middle ☐Indicated Point ☐Split Key Used: ☐ 1 ☐ 2 ☐ 3 ☐ 4 ☐ 5 ☐ 6 ☐ 7	_____

Account: _____	Additional Notes:
Username:	_____
Password:	_____
Secret Key: ☐Start ☐End ☐Middle ☐Indicated Point ☐Split Key Used: ☐ 1 ☐ 2 ☐ 3 ☐ 4 ☐ 5 ☐ 6 ☐ 7	_____

Account: _____	Additional Notes:
Username:	_____
Password:	_____
Secret Key: ☐Start ☐End ☐Middle ☐Indicated Point ☐Split Key Used: ☐ 1 ☐ 2 ☐ 3 ☐ 4 ☐ 5 ☐ 6 ☐ 7	_____

Account: _____	Additional Notes:
Username:	_____
Password:	_____
Secret Key: ☐Start ☐End ☐Middle ☐Indicated Point ☐Split Key Used: ☐ 1 ☐ 2 ☐ 3 ☐ 4 ☐ 5 ☐ 6 ☐ 7	_____

Account: _____	Additional Notes:
Username:	_____
Password:	_____
Secret Key: ☐Start ☐End ☐Middle ☐Indicated Point ☐Split Key Used: ☐ 1 ☐ 2 ☐ 3 ☐ 4 ☐ 5 ☐ 6 ☐ 7	_____

Account: _____ Additional Notes:

Username: _____ _____

Password: _____ _____

Secret Key: ☐Start ☐End ☐Middle ☐Indicated Point ☐Split
Key Used: ☐ 1 ☐ 2 ☐ 3 ☐ 4 ☐ 5 ☐ 6 ☐ 7 _____

Account: _____ Additional Notes:

Username: _____ _____

Password: _____ _____

Secret Key: ☐Start ☐End ☐Middle ☐Indicated Point ☐Split
Key Used: ☐ 1 ☐ 2 ☐ 3 ☐ 4 ☐ 5 ☐ 6 ☐ 7 _____

Account: _____ Additional Notes:

Username: _____ _____

Password: _____ _____

Secret Key: ☐Start ☐End ☐Middle ☐Indicated Point ☐Split
Key Used: ☐ 1 ☐ 2 ☐ 3 ☐ 4 ☐ 5 ☐ 6 ☐ 7 _____

Account: _____ Additional Notes:

Username: _____ _____

Password: _____ _____

Secret Key: ☐Start ☐End ☐Middle ☐Indicated Point ☐Split
Key Used: ☐ 1 ☐ 2 ☐ 3 ☐ 4 ☐ 5 ☐ 6 ☐ 7 _____

Account: _____ Additional Notes:

Username: _____ _____

Password: _____ _____

Secret Key: ☐Start ☐End ☐Middle ☐Indicated Point ☐Split
Key Used: ☐ 1 ☐ 2 ☐ 3 ☐ 4 ☐ 5 ☐ 6 ☐ 7 _____

Account: _____	Additional Notes:
Username: _____	_____
Password: _____	_____
Secret Key: □Start □End □Middle □Indicated Point □Split Key Used: □1 □2 □3 □4 □5 □6 □7	_____

Account: _____	Additional Notes:
Username: _____	_____
Password: _____	_____
Secret Key: □Start □End □Middle □Indicated Point □Split Key Used: □1 □2 □3 □4 □5 □6 □7	_____

Account: _____	Additional Notes:
Username: _____	_____
Password: _____	_____
Secret Key: □Start □End □Middle □Indicated Point □Split Key Used: □1 □2 □3 □4 □5 □6 □7	_____

Account: _____	Additional Notes:
Username: _____	_____
Password: _____	_____
Secret Key: □Start □End □Middle □Indicated Point □Split Key Used: □1 □2 □3 □4 □5 □6 □7	_____

Account: _____	Additional Notes:
Username: _____	_____
Password: _____	_____
Secret Key: □Start □End □Middle □Indicated Point □Split Key Used: □1 □2 □3 □4 □5 □6 □7	_____

Account: _____   Additional Notes:

Username: _____

Password: _____   _____

Secret Key: ☐Start ☐End ☐Middle ☐Indicated Point ☐Split
Key Used: ☐ 1 ☐ 2 ☐ 3 ☐ 4 ☐ 5 ☐ 6 ☐ 7   _____

Account: _____   Additional Notes:

Username: _____

Password: _____   _____

Secret Key: ☐Start ☐End ☐Middle ☐Indicated Point ☐Split
Key Used: ☐ 1 ☐ 2 ☐ 3 ☐ 4 ☐ 5 ☐ 6 ☐ 7   _____

Account: _____   Additional Notes:

Username: _____

Password: _____   _____

Secret Key: ☐Start ☐End ☐Middle ☐Indicated Point ☐Split
Key Used: ☐ 1 ☐ 2 ☐ 3 ☐ 4 ☐ 5 ☐ 6 ☐ 7   _____

Account: _____   Additional Notes:

Username: _____

Password: _____   _____

Secret Key: ☐Start ☐End ☐Middle ☐Indicated Point ☐Split
Key Used: ☐ 1 ☐ 2 ☐ 3 ☐ 4 ☐ 5 ☐ 6 ☐ 7   _____

Account: _____   Additional Notes:

Username: _____

Password: _____   _____

Secret Key: ☐Start ☐End ☐Middle ☐Indicated Point ☐Split
Key Used: ☐ 1 ☐ 2 ☐ 3 ☐ 4 ☐ 5 ☐ 6 ☐ 7   _____

U

Account: _____   Additional Notes:
Username: _____   _____
Password: _____   _____
Secret Key: ☐Start ☐End ☐Middle ☐Indicated Point ☐Split   _____
Key Used: ☐1 ☐2 ☐3 ☐4 ☐5 ☐6 ☐7

Account: _____   Additional Notes:
Username: _____   _____
Password: _____   _____
Secret Key: ☐Start ☐End ☐Middle ☐Indicated Point ☐Split   _____
Key Used: ☐1 ☐2 ☐3 ☐4 ☐5 ☐6 ☐7

Account: _____   Additional Notes:
Username: _____   _____
Password: _____   _____
Secret Key: ☐Start ☐End ☐Middle ☐Indicated Point ☐Split   _____
Key Used: ☐1 ☐2 ☐3 ☐4 ☐5 ☐6 ☐7

Account: _____   Additional Notes:
Username: _____   _____
Password: _____   _____
Secret Key: ☐Start ☐End ☐Middle ☐Indicated Point ☐Split   _____
Key Used: ☐1 ☐2 ☐3 ☐4 ☐5 ☐6 ☐7

Account: _____   Additional Notes:
Username: _____   _____
Password: _____   _____
Secret Key: ☐Start ☐End ☐Middle ☐Indicated Point ☐Split   _____
Key Used: ☐1 ☐2 ☐3 ☐4 ☐5 ☐6 ☐7

Account: _____ Additional Notes:

Username: _____ _____

Password: _____ _____

Secret Key: ☐Start ☐End ☐Middle ☐Indicated Point ☐Split
Key Used: ☐ 1 ☐ 2 ☐ 3 ☐ 4 ☐ 5 ☐ 6 ☐ 7 _____

Account: _____ Additional Notes:

Username: _____ _____

Password: _____ _____

Secret Key: ☐Start ☐End ☐Middle ☐Indicated Point ☐Split
Key Used: ☐ 1 ☐ 2 ☐ 3 ☐ 4 ☐ 5 ☐ 6 ☐ 7 _____

Account: _____ Additional Notes:

Username: _____ _____

Password: _____ _____

Secret Key: ☐Start ☐End ☐Middle ☐Indicated Point ☐Split
Key Used: ☐ 1 ☐ 2 ☐ 3 ☐ 4 ☐ 5 ☐ 6 ☐ 7 _____

Account: _____ Additional Notes:

Username: _____ _____

Password: _____ _____

Secret Key: ☐Start ☐End ☐Middle ☐Indicated Point ☐Split
Key Used: ☐ 1 ☐ 2 ☐ 3 ☐ 4 ☐ 5 ☐ 6 ☐ 7 _____

Account: _____ Additional Notes:

Username: _____ _____

Password: _____ _____

Secret Key: ☐Start ☐End ☐Middle ☐Indicated Point ☐Split
Key Used: ☐ 1 ☐ 2 ☐ 3 ☐ 4 ☐ 5 ☐ 6 ☐ 7 _____

Account: _____	Additional Notes:
Username: _____	_____
Password: _____	_____
Secret Key: ☐Start ☐End ☐Middle ☐Indicated Point ☐Split	_____
Key Used: ☐ 1 ☐ 2 ☐ 3 ☐ 4 ☐ 5 ☐ 6 ☐ 7	

Account: _____	Additional Notes:
Username: _____	_____
Password: _____	_____
Secret Key: ☐Start ☐End ☐Middle ☐Indicated Point ☐Split	_____
Key Used: ☐ 1 ☐ 2 ☐ 3 ☐ 4 ☐ 5 ☐ 6 ☐ 7	

Account: _____	Additional Notes:
Username: _____	_____
Password: _____	_____
Secret Key: ☐Start ☐End ☐Middle ☐Indicated Point ☐Split	_____
Key Used: ☐ 1 ☐ 2 ☐ 3 ☐ 4 ☐ 5 ☐ 6 ☐ 7	

Account: _____	Additional Notes:
Username: _____	_____
Password: _____	_____
Secret Key: ☐Start ☐End ☐Middle ☐Indicated Point ☐Split	_____
Key Used: ☐ 1 ☐ 2 ☐ 3 ☐ 4 ☐ 5 ☐ 6 ☐ 7	

Account: _____	Additional Notes:
Username: _____	_____
Password: _____	_____
Secret Key: ☐Start ☐End ☐Middle ☐Indicated Point ☐Split	_____
Key Used: ☐ 1 ☐ 2 ☐ 3 ☐ 4 ☐ 5 ☐ 6 ☐ 7	

The Encrypted Book of Passwords

Account: _____	Additional Notes:
Username: _____	_____
Password: _____	_____
Secret Key: ☐Start ☐End ☐Middle ☐Indicated Point ☐Split Key Used: ☐ 1 ☐ 2 ☐ 3 ☐ 4 ☐ 5 ☐ 6 ☐ 7	_____

Account: _____	Additional Notes:
Username: _____	_____
Password: _____	_____
Secret Key: ☐Start ☐End ☐Middle ☐Indicated Point ☐Split Key Used: ☐ 1 ☐ 2 ☐ 3 ☐ 4 ☐ 5 ☐ 6 ☐ 7	_____

Account: _____	Additional Notes:
Username: _____	_____
Password: _____	_____
Secret Key: ☐Start ☐End ☐Middle ☐Indicated Point ☐Split Key Used: ☐ 1 ☐ 2 ☐ 3 ☐ 4 ☐ 5 ☐ 6 ☐ 7	_____

Account: _____	Additional Notes:
Username: _____	_____
Password: _____	_____
Secret Key: ☐Start ☐End ☐Middle ☐Indicated Point ☐Split Key Used: ☐ 1 ☐ 2 ☐ 3 ☐ 4 ☐ 5 ☐ 6 ☐ 7	_____

Account: _____	Additional Notes:
Username: _____	_____
Password: _____	_____
Secret Key: ☐Start ☐End ☐Middle ☐Indicated Point ☐Split Key Used: ☐ 1 ☐ 2 ☐ 3 ☐ 4 ☐ 5 ☐ 6 ☐ 7	_____

V

Account: _____	Additional Notes:
Username: _____	_____
Password: _____	_____
Secret Key: ☐Start ☐End ☐Middle ☐Indicated Point ☐Split Key Used: ☐ 1 ☐ 2 ☐ 3 ☐ 4 ☐ 5 ☐ 6 ☐ 7	_____

Account: _____	Additional Notes:
Username: _____	_____
Password: _____	_____
Secret Key: ☐Start ☐End ☐Middle ☐Indicated Point ☐Split Key Used: ☐ 1 ☐ 2 ☐ 3 ☐ 4 ☐ 5 ☐ 6 ☐ 7	_____

Account: _____	Additional Notes:
Username: _____	_____
Password: _____	_____
Secret Key: ☐Start ☐End ☐Middle ☐Indicated Point ☐Split Key Used: ☐ 1 ☐ 2 ☐ 3 ☐ 4 ☐ 5 ☐ 6 ☐ 7	_____

Account: _____	Additional Notes:
Username: _____	_____
Password: _____	_____
Secret Key: ☐Start ☐End ☐Middle ☐Indicated Point ☐Split Key Used: ☐ 1 ☐ 2 ☐ 3 ☐ 4 ☐ 5 ☐ 6 ☐ 7	_____

Account: _____	Additional Notes:
Username: _____	_____
Password: _____	_____
Secret Key: ☐Start ☐End ☐Middle ☐Indicated Point ☐Split Key Used: ☐ 1 ☐ 2 ☐ 3 ☐ 4 ☐ 5 ☐ 6 ☐ 7	_____

Account: _____   Additional Notes:

Username: _____   _____

Password: _____   _____

Secret Key: ☐Start ☐End ☐Middle ☐Indicated Point ☐Split   _____
Key Used: ☐ 1 ☐ 2 ☐ 3 ☐ 4 ☐ 5 ☐ 6 ☐ 7

Account: _____   Additional Notes:

Username: _____   _____

Password: _____   _____

Secret Key: ☐Start ☐End ☐Middle ☐Indicated Point ☐Split   _____
Key Used: ☐ 1 ☐ 2 ☐ 3 ☐ 4 ☐ 5 ☐ 6 ☐ 7

Account: _____   Additional Notes:

Username: _____   _____

Password: _____   _____

Secret Key: ☐Start ☐End ☐Middle ☐Indicated Point ☐Split   _____
Key Used: ☐ 1 ☐ 2 ☐ 3 ☐ 4 ☐ 5 ☐ 6 ☐ 7

Account: _____   Additional Notes:

Username: _____   _____

Password: _____   _____

Secret Key: ☐Start ☐End ☐Middle ☐Indicated Point ☐Split   _____
Key Used: ☐ 1 ☐ 2 ☐ 3 ☐ 4 ☐ 5 ☐ 6 ☐ 7

Account: _____   Additional Notes:

Username: _____   _____

Password: _____   _____

Secret Key: ☐Start ☐End ☐Middle ☐Indicated Point ☐Split   _____
Key Used: ☐ 1 ☐ 2 ☐ 3 ☐ 4 ☐ 5 ☐ 6 ☐ 7

Account: _____	Additional Notes:
Username: _____	_____
Password: _____	_____
Secret Key: □Start □End □Middle □Indicated Point □Split Key Used: □ 1 □ 2 □ 3 □ 4 □ 5 □ 6 □ 7	_____

Account: _____	Additional Notes:
Username: _____	_____
Password: _____	_____
Secret Key: □Start □End □Middle □Indicated Point □Split Key Used: □ 1 □ 2 □ 3 □ 4 □ 5 □ 6 □ 7	_____

Account: _____	Additional Notes:
Username: _____	_____
Password: _____	_____
Secret Key: □Start □End □Middle □Indicated Point □Split Key Used: □ 1 □ 2 □ 3 □ 4 □ 5 □ 6 □ 7	_____

Account: _____	Additional Notes:
Username: _____	_____
Password: _____	_____
Secret Key: □Start □End □Middle □Indicated Point □Split Key Used: □ 1 □ 2 □ 3 □ 4 □ 5 □ 6 □ 7	_____

Account: _____	Additional Notes:
Username: _____	_____
Password: _____	_____
Secret Key: □Start □End □Middle □Indicated Point □Split Key Used: □ 1 □ 2 □ 3 □ 4 □ 5 □ 6 □ 7	_____

The Encrypted Book of Passwords

Account: _____   Additional Notes:

Username: _____   _____

Password: _____   _____

Secret Key: ☐Start ☐End ☐Middle ☐Indicated Point ☐Split   _____
Key Used: ☐ 1 ☐ 2 ☐ 3 ☐ 4 ☐ 5 ☐ 6 ☐ 7

Account: _____   Additional Notes:

Username: _____   _____

Password: _____   _____

Secret Key: ☐Start ☐End ☐Middle ☐Indicated Point ☐Split   _____
Key Used: ☐ 1 ☐ 2 ☐ 3 ☐ 4 ☐ 5 ☐ 6 ☐ 7

Account: _____   Additional Notes:

Username: _____   _____

Password: _____   _____

Secret Key: ☐Start ☐End ☐Middle ☐Indicated Point ☐Split   _____
Key Used: ☐ 1 ☐ 2 ☐ 3 ☐ 4 ☐ 5 ☐ 6 ☐ 7

Account: _____   Additional Notes:

Username: _____   _____

Password: _____   _____

Secret Key: ☐Start ☐End ☐Middle ☐Indicated Point ☐Split   _____
Key Used: ☐ 1 ☐ 2 ☐ 3 ☐ 4 ☐ 5 ☐ 6 ☐ 7

Account: _____   Additional Notes:

Username: _____   _____

Password: _____   _____

Secret Key: ☐Start ☐End ☐Middle ☐Indicated Point ☐Split   _____
Key Used: ☐ 1 ☐ 2 ☐ 3 ☐ 4 ☐ 5 ☐ 6 ☐ 7

W

Account: _____	Additional Notes:
Username: _____	_____
Password: _____	_____
Secret Key: ☐Start ☐End ☐Middle ☐Indicated Point ☐Split	_____
Key Used: ☐ 1 ☐ 2 ☐ 3 ☐ 4 ☐ 5 ☐ 6 ☐ 7	

Account: _____	Additional Notes:
Username: _____	_____
Password: _____	_____
Secret Key: ☐Start ☐End ☐Middle ☐Indicated Point ☐Split	_____
Key Used: ☐ 1 ☐ 2 ☐ 3 ☐ 4 ☐ 5 ☐ 6 ☐ 7	

Account: _____	Additional Notes:
Username: _____	_____
Password: _____	_____
Secret Key: ☐Start ☐End ☐Middle ☐Indicated Point ☐Split	_____
Key Used: ☐ 1 ☐ 2 ☐ 3 ☐ 4 ☐ 5 ☐ 6 ☐ 7	

Account: _____	Additional Notes:
Username: _____	_____
Password: _____	_____
Secret Key: ☐Start ☐End ☐Middle ☐Indicated Point ☐Split	_____
Key Used: ☐ 1 ☐ 2 ☐ 3 ☐ 4 ☐ 5 ☐ 6 ☐ 7	

Account: _____	Additional Notes:
Username: _____	_____
Password: _____	_____
Secret Key: ☐Start ☐End ☐Middle ☐Indicated Point ☐Split	_____
Key Used: ☐ 1 ☐ 2 ☐ 3 ☐ 4 ☐ 5 ☐ 6 ☐ 7	

Account: _____ Additional Notes:

Username: _____ _____

Password: _____ _____

Secret Key: ☐Start ☐End ☐Middle ☐Indicated Point ☐Split
Key Used: ☐ 1 ☐ 2 ☐ 3 ☐ 4 ☐ 5☐ 6 ☐ 7   _____

Account: _____ Additional Notes:

Username: _____ _____

Password: _____ _____

Secret Key: ☐Start ☐End ☐Middle ☐Indicated Point ☐Split
Key Used: ☐ 1 ☐ 2 ☐ 3 ☐ 4 ☐ 5☐ 6 ☐ 7   _____

Account: _____ Additional Notes:

Username: _____ _____

Password: _____ _____

Secret Key: ☐Start ☐End ☐Middle ☐Indicated Point ☐Split
Key Used: ☐ 1 ☐ 2 ☐ 3 ☐ 4 ☐ 5☐ 6 ☐ 7   _____

Account: _____ Additional Notes:

Username: _____ _____

Password: _____ _____

Secret Key: ☐Start ☐End ☐Middle ☐Indicated Point ☐Split
Key Used: ☐ 1 ☐ 2 ☐ 3 ☐ 4 ☐ 5☐ 6 ☐ 7   _____

Account: _____ Additional Notes:

Username: _____ _____

Password: _____ _____

Secret Key: ☐Start ☐End ☐Middle ☐Indicated Point ☐Split
Key Used: ☐ 1 ☐ 2 ☐ 3 ☐ 4 ☐ 5☐ 6 ☐ 7   _____

Account: _____	Additional Notes:
Username: _____	_____
Password: _____	_____
Secret Key: ☐Start ☐End ☐Middle ☐Indicated Point ☐Split Key Used: ☐ 1 ☐ 2 ☐ 3 ☐ 4 ☐ 5 ☐ 6 ☐ 7	_____

Account: _____	Additional Notes:
Username: _____	_____
Password: _____	_____
Secret Key: ☐Start ☐End ☐Middle ☐Indicated Point ☐Split Key Used: ☐ 1 ☐ 2 ☐ 3 ☐ 4 ☐ 5 ☐ 6 ☐ 7	_____

Account: _____	Additional Notes:
Username: _____	_____
Password: _____	_____
Secret Key: ☐Start ☐End ☐Middle ☐Indicated Point ☐Split Key Used: ☐ 1 ☐ 2 ☐ 3 ☐ 4 ☐ 5 ☐ 6 ☐ 7	_____

Account: _____	Additional Notes:
Username: _____	_____
Password: _____	_____
Secret Key: ☐Start ☐End ☐Middle ☐Indicated Point ☐Split Key Used: ☐ 1 ☐ 2 ☐ 3 ☐ 4 ☐ 5 ☐ 6 ☐ 7	_____

Account: _____	Additional Notes:
Username: _____	_____
Password: _____	_____
Secret Key: ☐Start ☐End ☐Middle ☐Indicated Point ☐Split Key Used: ☐ 1 ☐ 2 ☐ 3 ☐ 4 ☐ 5 ☐ 6 ☐ 7	_____

Account: _____   Additional Notes:

Username: _____   _____

Password: _____   _____

Secret Key: ☐Start ☐End ☐Middle ☐Indicated Point ☐Split
Key Used: ☐ 1 ☐ 2 ☐ 3 ☐ 4 ☐ 5 ☐ 6 ☐ 7   _____

Account: _____   Additional Notes:

Username: _____   _____

Password: _____   _____

Secret Key: ☐Start ☐End ☐Middle ☐Indicated Point ☐Split
Key Used: ☐ 1 ☐ 2 ☐ 3 ☐ 4 ☐ 5 ☐ 6 ☐ 7   _____

Account: _____   Additional Notes:

Username: _____   _____

Password: _____   _____

Secret Key: ☐Start ☐End ☐Middle ☐Indicated Point ☐Split
Key Used: ☐ 1 ☐ 2 ☐ 3 ☐ 4 ☐ 5 ☐ 6 ☐ 7   _____

Account: _____   Additional Notes:

Username: _____   _____

Password: _____   _____

Secret Key: ☐Start ☐End ☐Middle ☐Indicated Point ☐Split
Key Used: ☐ 1 ☐ 2 ☐ 3 ☐ 4 ☐ 5 ☐ 6 ☐ 7   _____

Account: _____   Additional Notes:

Username: _____   _____

Password: _____   _____

Secret Key: ☐Start ☐End ☐Middle ☐Indicated Point ☐Split
Key Used: ☐ 1 ☐ 2 ☐ 3 ☐ 4 ☐ 5 ☐ 6 ☐ 7   _____

X

Account: _____	Additional Notes:
Username: _____	_____
Password: _____	_____
Secret Key: ☐Start ☐End ☐Middle ☐Indicated Point ☐Split Key Used: ☐ 1 ☐ 2 ☐ 3 ☐ 4 ☐ 5 ☐ 6 ☐ 7	_____

Account: _____	Additional Notes:
Username: _____	_____
Password: _____	_____
Secret Key: ☐Start ☐End ☐Middle ☐Indicated Point ☐Split Key Used: ☐ 1 ☐ 2 ☐ 3 ☐ 4 ☐ 5 ☐ 6 ☐ 7	_____

Account: _____	Additional Notes:
Username: _____	_____
Password: _____	_____
Secret Key: ☐Start ☐End ☐Middle ☐Indicated Point ☐Split Key Used: ☐ 1 ☐ 2 ☐ 3 ☐ 4 ☐ 5 ☐ 6 ☐ 7	_____

Account: _____	Additional Notes:
Username: _____	_____
Password: _____	_____
Secret Key: ☐Start ☐End ☐Middle ☐Indicated Point ☐Split Key Used: ☐ 1 ☐ 2 ☐ 3 ☐ 4 ☐ 5 ☐ 6 ☐ 7	_____

Account: _____	Additional Notes:
Username: _____	_____
Password: _____	_____
Secret Key: ☐Start ☐End ☐Middle ☐Indicated Point ☐Split Key Used: ☐ 1 ☐ 2 ☐ 3 ☐ 4 ☐ 5 ☐ 6 ☐ 7	_____

Account: _____   Additional Notes:

Username: _____

Password: _____

Secret Key: ☐Start ☐End ☐Middle ☐Indicated Point ☐Split
Key Used: ☐ 1 ☐ 2 ☐ 3 ☐ 4 ☐ 5 ☐ 6 ☐ 7

Account: _____   Additional Notes:

Username: _____

Password: _____

Secret Key: ☐Start ☐End ☐Middle ☐Indicated Point ☐Split
Key Used: ☐ 1 ☐ 2 ☐ 3 ☐ 4 ☐ 5 ☐ 6 ☐ 7

Account: _____   Additional Notes:

Username: _____

Password: _____

Secret Key: ☐Start ☐End ☐Middle ☐Indicated Point ☐Split
Key Used: ☐ 1 ☐ 2 ☐ 3 ☐ 4 ☐ 5 ☐ 6 ☐ 7

Account: _____   Additional Notes:

Username: _____

Password: _____

Secret Key: ☐Start ☐End ☐Middle ☐Indicated Point ☐Split
Key Used: ☐ 1 ☐ 2 ☐ 3 ☐ 4 ☐ 5 ☐ 6 ☐ 7

Account: _____   Additional Notes:

Username: _____

Password: _____

Secret Key: ☐Start ☐End ☐Middle ☐Indicated Point ☐Split
Key Used: ☐ 1 ☐ 2 ☐ 3 ☐ 4 ☐ 5 ☐ 6 ☐ 7

Y

Account: _____	Additional Notes:
Username: _____	_____
Password: _____	_____
Secret Key: □Start □End □Middle □Indicated Point □Split Key Used: □ 1 □ 2 □ 3 □ 4 □ 5 □ 6 □ 7	_____

Account: _____	Additional Notes:
Username: _____	_____
Password: _____	_____
Secret Key: □Start □End □Middle □Indicated Point □Split Key Used: □ 1 □ 2 □ 3 □ 4 □ 5 □ 6 □ 7	_____

Account: _____	Additional Notes:
Username: _____	_____
Password: _____	_____
Secret Key: □Start □End □Middle □Indicated Point □Split Key Used: □ 1 □ 2 □ 3 □ 4 □ 5 □ 6 □ 7	_____

Account: _____	Additional Notes:
Username: _____	_____
Password: _____	_____
Secret Key: □Start □End □Middle □Indicated Point □Split Key Used: □ 1 □ 2 □ 3 □ 4 □ 5 □ 6 □ 7	_____

Account: _____	Additional Notes:
Username: _____	_____
Password: _____	_____
Secret Key: □Start □End □Middle □Indicated Point □Split Key Used: □ 1 □ 2 □ 3 □ 4 □ 5 □ 6 □ 7	_____

Account: _____   Additional Notes:

Username: _____

Password: _____   _____

Secret Key: ☐Start ☐End ☐Middle ☐Indicated Point ☐Split
Key Used: ☐ 1 ☐ 2 ☐ 3 ☐ 4 ☐ 5 ☐ 6 ☐ 7   _____

Account: _____   Additional Notes:

Username: _____

Password: _____   _____

Secret Key: ☐Start ☐End ☐Middle ☐Indicated Point ☐Split
Key Used: ☐ 1 ☐ 2 ☐ 3 ☐ 4 ☐ 5 ☐ 6 ☐ 7   _____

Account: _____   Additional Notes:

Username: _____

Password: _____   _____

Secret Key: ☐Start ☐End ☐Middle ☐Indicated Point ☐Split
Key Used: ☐ 1 ☐ 2 ☐ 3 ☐ 4 ☐ 5 ☐ 6 ☐ 7   _____

Account: _____   Additional Notes:

Username: _____

Password: _____   _____

Secret Key: ☐Start ☐End ☐Middle ☐Indicated Point ☐Split
Key Used: ☐ 1 ☐ 2 ☐ 3 ☐ 4 ☐ 5 ☐ 6 ☐ 7   _____

Account: _____   Additional Notes:

Username: _____

Password: _____   _____

Secret Key: ☐Start ☐End ☐Middle ☐Indicated Point ☐Split
Key Used: ☐ 1 ☐ 2 ☐ 3 ☐ 4 ☐ 5 ☐ 6 ☐ 7   _____

Account: _____ Additional Notes:

Username: _____ _____

Password: _____ _____

Secret Key: ☐Start ☐End ☐Middle ☐Indicated Point ☐Split
Key Used: ☐ 1 ☐ 2 ☐ 3 ☐ 4 ☐ 5 ☐ 6 ☐ 7 _____

Account: _____ Additional Notes:

Username: _____ _____

Password: _____ _____

Secret Key: ☐Start ☐End ☐Middle ☐Indicated Point ☐Split
Key Used: ☐ 1 ☐ 2 ☐ 3 ☐ 4 ☐ 5 ☐ 6 ☐ 7 _____

Account: _____ Additional Notes:

Username: _____ _____

Password: _____ _____

Secret Key: ☐Start ☐End ☐Middle ☐Indicated Point ☐Split
Key Used: ☐ 1 ☐ 2 ☐ 3 ☐ 4 ☐ 5 ☐ 6 ☐ 7 _____

Account: _____ Additional Notes:

Username: _____ _____

Password: _____ _____

Secret Key: ☐Start ☐End ☐Middle ☐Indicated Point ☐Split
Key Used: ☐ 1 ☐ 2 ☐ 3 ☐ 4 ☐ 5 ☐ 6 ☐ 7 _____

Account: _____ Additional Notes:

Username: _____ _____

Password: _____ _____

Secret Key: ☐Start ☐End ☐Middle ☐Indicated Point ☐Split
Key Used: ☐ 1 ☐ 2 ☐ 3 ☐ 4 ☐ 5 ☐ 6 ☐ 7 _____

Account: _____   Additional Notes:

Username: _____   _____

Password: _____   _____

Secret Key: ☐Start ☐End ☐Middle ☐Indicated Point ☐Split
Key Used: ☐ 1 ☐ 2 ☐ 3 ☐ 4 ☐ 5 ☐ 6 ☐ 7   _____

Account: _____   Additional Notes:

Username: _____   _____

Password: _____   _____

Secret Key: ☐Start ☐End ☐Middle ☐Indicated Point ☐Split
Key Used: ☐ 1 ☐ 2 ☐ 3 ☐ 4 ☐ 5 ☐ 6 ☐ 7   _____

Account: _____   Additional Notes:

Username: _____   _____

Password: _____   _____

Secret Key: ☐Start ☐End ☐Middle ☐Indicated Point ☐Split
Key Used: ☐ 1 ☐ 2 ☐ 3 ☐ 4 ☐ 5 ☐ 6 ☐ 7   _____

Account: _____   Additional Notes:

Username: _____   _____

Password: _____   _____

Secret Key: ☐Start ☐End ☐Middle ☐Indicated Point ☐Split
Key Used: ☐ 1 ☐ 2 ☐ 3 ☐ 4 ☐ 5 ☐ 6 ☐ 7   _____

Account: _____   Additional Notes:

Username: _____   _____

Password: _____   _____

Secret Key: ☐Start ☐End ☐Middle ☐Indicated Point ☐Split
Key Used: ☐ 1 ☐ 2 ☐ 3 ☐ 4 ☐ 5 ☐ 6 ☐ 7   _____

Z

Account: _____	Additional Notes:
Username: _____	_____
Password: _____	_____
Secret Key: ☐Start ☐End ☐Middle ☐Indicated Point ☐Split	_____
Key Used: ☐ 1 ☐ 2 ☐ 3 ☐ 4 ☐ 5 ☐ 6 ☐ 7	

Account: _____	Additional Notes:
Username: _____	_____
Password: _____	_____
Secret Key: ☐Start ☐End ☐Middle ☐Indicated Point ☐Split	_____
Key Used: ☐ 1 ☐ 2 ☐ 3 ☐ 4 ☐ 5 ☐ 6 ☐ 7	

Account: _____	Additional Notes:
Username: _____	_____
Password: _____	_____
Secret Key: ☐Start ☐End ☐Middle ☐Indicated Point ☐Split	_____
Key Used: ☐ 1 ☐ 2 ☐ 3 ☐ 4 ☐ 5 ☐ 6 ☐ 7	

Account: _____	Additional Notes:
Username: _____	_____
Password: _____	_____
Secret Key: ☐Start ☐End ☐Middle ☐Indicated Point ☐Split	_____
Key Used: ☐ 1 ☐ 2 ☐ 3 ☐ 4 ☐ 5 ☐ 6 ☐ 7	

Account: _____	Additional Notes:
Username: _____	_____
Password: _____	_____
Secret Key: ☐Start ☐End ☐Middle ☐Indicated Point ☐Split	_____
Key Used: ☐ 1 ☐ 2 ☐ 3 ☐ 4 ☐ 5 ☐ 6 ☐ 7	

Account: _____ Additional Notes:

Username: _____ _____

Password: _____ _____

Secret Key: ☐Start ☐End ☐Middle ☐Indicated Point ☐Split _____
Key Used: ☐ 1 ☐ 2 ☐ 3 ☐ 4 ☐ 5 ☐ 6 ☐ 7

Account: _____ Additional Notes:

Username: _____ _____

Password: _____ _____

Secret Key: ☐Start ☐End ☐Middle ☐Indicated Point ☐Split _____
Key Used: ☐ 1 ☐ 2 ☐ 3 ☐ 4 ☐ 5 ☐ 6 ☐ 7

Account: _____ Additional Notes:

Username: _____ _____

Password: _____ _____

Secret Key: ☐Start ☐End ☐Middle ☐Indicated Point ☐Split _____
Key Used: ☐ 1 ☐ 2 ☐ 3 ☐ 4 ☐ 5 ☐ 6 ☐ 7

Account: _____ Additional Notes:

Username: _____ _____

Password: _____ _____

Secret Key: ☐Start ☐End ☐Middle ☐Indicated Point ☐Split _____
Key Used: ☐ 1 ☐ 2 ☐ 3 ☐ 4 ☐ 5 ☐ 6 ☐ 7

Account: _____ Additional Notes:

Username: _____ _____

Password: _____ _____

Secret Key: ☐Start ☐End ☐Middle ☐Indicated Point ☐Split _____
Key Used: ☐ 1 ☐ 2 ☐ 3 ☐ 4 ☐ 5 ☐ 6 ☐ 7

Account: _____	Additional Notes:
Username: _____	_____
Password: _____	_____
Secret Key: ☐Start ☐End ☐Middle ☐Indicated Point ☐Split Key Used: ☐1 ☐2 ☐3 ☐4 ☐5 ☐6 ☐7	_____

Account: _____	Additional Notes:
Username: _____	_____
Password: _____	_____
Secret Key: ☐Start ☐End ☐Middle ☐Indicated Point ☐Split Key Used: ☐1 ☐2 ☐3 ☐4 ☐5 ☐6 ☐7	_____

Account: _____	Additional Notes:
Username: _____	_____
Password: _____	_____
Secret Key: ☐Start ☐End ☐Middle ☐Indicated Point ☐Split Key Used: ☐1 ☐2 ☐3 ☐4 ☐5 ☐6 ☐7	_____

Account: _____	Additional Notes:
Username: _____	_____
Password: _____	_____
Secret Key: ☐Start ☐End ☐Middle ☐Indicated Point ☐Split Key Used: ☐1 ☐2 ☐3 ☐4 ☐5 ☐6 ☐7	_____

Account: _____	Additional Notes:
Username: _____	_____
Password: _____	_____
Secret Key: ☐Start ☐End ☐Middle ☐Indicated Point ☐Split Key Used: ☐1 ☐2 ☐3 ☐4 ☐5 ☐6 ☐7	_____

The Encrypted Book of Passwords

Account: _____ Additional Notes:

Username: _____ _____

Password: _____ _____

Secret Key: □Start □End □Middle □Indicated Point □Split _____
Key Used: □ 1 □ 2 □ 3 □ 4 □ 5 □ 6 □ 7

Account: _____ Additional Notes:

Username: _____ _____

Password: _____ _____

Secret Key: □Start □End □Middle □Indicated Point □Split _____
Key Used: □ 1 □ 2 □ 3 □ 4 □ 5 □ 6 □ 7

Account: _____ Additional Notes:

Username: _____ _____

Password: _____ _____

Secret Key: □Start □End □Middle □Indicated Point □Split _____
Key Used: □ 1 □ 2 □ 3 □ 4 □ 5 □ 6 □ 7

Account: _____ Additional Notes:

Username: _____ _____

Password: _____ _____

Secret Key: □Start □End □Middle □Indicated Point □Split _____
Key Used: □ 1 □ 2 □ 3 □ 4 □ 5 □ 6 □ 7

Account: _____ Additional Notes:

Username: _____ _____

Password: _____ _____

Secret Key: □Start □End □Middle □Indicated Point □Split _____
Key Used: □ 1 □ 2 □ 3 □ 4 □ 5 □ 6 □ 7

Other Accounts

Account: _____   Additional Notes:

Username: _____   _____

Password: _____   _____

Secret Key: ☐Start ☐End ☐Middle ☐Indicated Point ☐Split
Key Used: ☐ 1 ☐ 2 ☐ 3 ☐ 4 ☐ 5 ☐ 6 ☐ 7   _____

Account: _____   Additional Notes:

Username: _____   _____

Password: _____   _____

Secret Key: ☐Start ☐End ☐Middle ☐Indicated Point ☐Split
Key Used: ☐ 1 ☐ 2 ☐ 3 ☐ 4 ☐ 5 ☐ 6 ☐ 7   _____

Account: _____   Additional Notes:

Username: _____   _____

Password: _____   _____

Secret Key: ☐Start ☐End ☐Middle ☐Indicated Point ☐Split
Key Used: ☐ 1 ☐ 2 ☐ 3 ☐ 4 ☐ 5 ☐ 6 ☐ 7   _____

Account: _____   Additional Notes:

Username: _____   _____

Password: _____   _____

Secret Key: ☐Start ☐End ☐Middle ☐Indicated Point ☐Split
Key Used: ☐ 1 ☐ 2 ☐ 3 ☐ 4 ☐ 5 ☐ 6 ☐ 7   _____

Account: _____   Additional Notes:

Username: _____   _____

Password: _____   _____

Secret Key: ☐Start ☐End ☐Middle ☐Indicated Point ☐Split
Key Used: ☐ 1 ☐ 2 ☐ 3 ☐ 4 ☐ 5 ☐ 6 ☐ 7   _____

The Encrypted Book of Passwords

Account: _____	Additional Notes:
Username: _____	_____
Password: _____	_____
Secret Key: ☐Start ☐End ☐Middle ☐Indicated Point ☐Split	_____
Key Used: ☐ 1 ☐ 2 ☐ 3 ☐ 4 ☐ 5 ☐ 6 ☐ 7	

Account: _____	Additional Notes:
Username: _____	_____
Password: _____	_____
Secret Key: ☐Start ☐End ☐Middle ☐Indicated Point ☐Split	_____
Key Used: ☐ 1 ☐ 2 ☐ 3 ☐ 4 ☐ 5 ☐ 6 ☐ 7	

Account: _____	Additional Notes:
Username: _____	_____
Password: _____	_____
Secret Key: ☐Start ☐End ☐Middle ☐Indicated Point ☐Split	_____
Key Used: ☐ 1 ☐ 2 ☐ 3 ☐ 4 ☐ 5 ☐ 6 ☐ 7	

Account: _____	Additional Notes:
Username: _____	_____
Password: _____	_____
Secret Key: ☐Start ☐End ☐Middle ☐Indicated Point ☐Split	_____
Key Used: ☐ 1 ☐ 2 ☐ 3 ☐ 4 ☐ 5 ☐ 6 ☐ 7	

Account: _____	Additional Notes:
Username: _____	_____
Password: _____	_____
Secret Key: ☐Start ☐End ☐Middle ☐Indicated Point ☐Split	_____
Key Used: ☐ 1 ☐ 2 ☐ 3 ☐ 4 ☐ 5 ☐ 6 ☐ 7	

Account: _____	Additional Notes:
Username: _____	_____
Password: _____	_____
Secret Key: ☐Start ☐End ☐Middle ☐Indicated Point ☐Split Key Used: ☐1 ☐2 ☐3 ☐4 ☐5 ☐6 ☐7	_____

Account: _____	Additional Notes:
Username: _____	_____
Password: _____	_____
Secret Key: ☐Start ☐End ☐Middle ☐Indicated Point ☐Split Key Used: ☐1 ☐2 ☐3 ☐4 ☐5 ☐6 ☐7	_____

Account: _____	Additional Notes:
Username: _____	_____
Password: _____	_____
Secret Key: ☐Start ☐End ☐Middle ☐Indicated Point ☐Split Key Used: ☐1 ☐2 ☐3 ☐4 ☐5 ☐6 ☐7	_____

Account: _____	Additional Notes:
Username: _____	_____
Password: _____	_____
Secret Key: ☐Start ☐End ☐Middle ☐Indicated Point ☐Split Key Used: ☐1 ☐2 ☐3 ☐4 ☐5 ☐6 ☐7	_____

Account: _____	Additional Notes:
Username: _____	_____
Password: _____	_____
Secret Key: ☐Start ☐End ☐Middle ☐Indicated Point ☐Split Key Used: ☐1 ☐2 ☐3 ☐4 ☐5 ☐6 ☐7	_____

Account: _____   Additional Notes:

Username: _____

Password: _____   _____

Secret Key: ☐Start ☐End ☐Middle ☐Indicated Point ☐Split
Key Used: ☐ 1 ☐ 2 ☐ 3 ☐ 4 ☐ 5 ☐ 6 ☐ 7   _____

Account: _____   Additional Notes:

Username: _____

Password: _____   _____

Secret Key: ☐Start ☐End ☐Middle ☐Indicated Point ☐Split
Key Used: ☐ 1 ☐ 2 ☐ 3 ☐ 4 ☐ 5 ☐ 6 ☐ 7   _____

Account: _____   Additional Notes:

Username: _____

Password: _____   _____

Secret Key: ☐Start ☐End ☐Middle ☐Indicated Point ☐Split
Key Used: ☐ 1 ☐ 2 ☐ 3 ☐ 4 ☐ 5 ☐ 6 ☐ 7   _____

Account: _____   Additional Notes:

Username: _____

Password: _____   _____

Secret Key: ☐Start ☐End ☐Middle ☐Indicated Point ☐Split
Key Used: ☐ 1 ☐ 2 ☐ 3 ☐ 4 ☐ 5 ☐ 6 ☐ 7   _____

Account: _____   Additional Notes:

Username: _____

Password: _____   _____

Secret Key: ☐Start ☐End ☐Middle ☐Indicated Point ☐Split
Key Used: ☐ 1 ☐ 2 ☐ 3 ☐ 4 ☐ 5 ☐ 6 ☐ 7   _____

Account: _____	Additional Notes:
Username: _____	_____
Password: _____	_____
Secret Key: □Start □End □Middle □Indicated Point □Split Key Used: □ 1 □ 2 □ 3 □ 4 □ 5 □ 6 □ 7	_____

Account: _____	Additional Notes:
Username: _____	_____
Password: _____	_____
Secret Key: □Start □End □Middle □Indicated Point □Split Key Used: □ 1 □ 2 □ 3 □ 4 □ 5 □ 6 □ 7	_____

Account: _____	Additional Notes:
Username: _____	_____
Password: _____	_____
Secret Key: □Start □End □Middle □Indicated Point □Split Key Used: □ 1 □ 2 □ 3 □ 4 □ 5 □ 6 □ 7	_____

Account: _____	Additional Notes:
Username: _____	_____
Password: _____	_____
Secret Key: □Start □End □Middle □Indicated Point □Split Key Used: □ 1 □ 2 □ 3 □ 4 □ 5 □ 6 □ 7	_____

Account: _____	Additional Notes:
Username: _____	_____
Password: _____	_____
Secret Key: □Start □End □Middle □Indicated Point □Split Key Used: □ 1 □ 2 □ 3 □ 4 □ 5 □ 6 □ 7	_____

Account: _____ Additional Notes:

Username: _____ _____

Password: _____ _____

Secret Key: ☐Start ☐End ☐Middle ☐Indicated Point ☐Split
Key Used: ☐ 1 ☐ 2 ☐ 3 ☐ 4 ☐ 5 ☐ 6 ☐ 7 _____

Account: _____ Additional Notes:

Username: _____ _____

Password: _____ _____

Secret Key: ☐Start ☐End ☐Middle ☐Indicated Point ☐Split
Key Used: ☐ 1 ☐ 2 ☐ 3 ☐ 4 ☐ 5 ☐ 6 ☐ 7 _____

Account: _____ Additional Notes:

Username: _____ _____

Password: _____ _____

Secret Key: ☐Start ☐End ☐Middle ☐Indicated Point ☐Split
Key Used: ☐ 1 ☐ 2 ☐ 3 ☐ 4 ☐ 5 ☐ 6 ☐ 7 _____

Account: _____ Additional Notes:

Username: _____ _____

Password: _____ _____

Secret Key: ☐Start ☐End ☐Middle ☐Indicated Point ☐Split
Key Used: ☐ 1 ☐ 2 ☐ 3 ☐ 4 ☐ 5 ☐ 6 ☐ 7 _____

Account: _____ Additional Notes:

Username: _____ _____

Password: _____ _____

Secret Key: ☐Start ☐End ☐Middle ☐Indicated Point ☐Split
Key Used: ☐ 1 ☐ 2 ☐ 3 ☐ 4 ☐ 5 ☐ 6 ☐ 7 _____

Account: _____   Additional Notes:

Username: _____   _____

Password: _____   _____

Secret Key: ☐Start ☐End ☐Middle ☐Indicated Point ☐Split   _____
Key Used: ☐ 1 ☐ 2 ☐ 3 ☐ 4 ☐ 5 ☐ 6 ☐ 7

Account: _____   Additional Notes:

Username: _____   _____

Password: _____   _____

Secret Key: ☐Start ☐End ☐Middle ☐Indicated Point ☐Split   _____
Key Used: ☐ 1 ☐ 2 ☐ 3 ☐ 4 ☐ 5 ☐ 6 ☐ 7

Account: _____   Additional Notes:

Username: _____   _____

Password: _____   _____

Secret Key: ☐Start ☐End ☐Middle ☐Indicated Point ☐Split   _____
Key Used: ☐ 1 ☐ 2 ☐ 3 ☐ 4 ☐ 5 ☐ 6 ☐ 7

Account: _____   Additional Notes:

Username: _____   _____

Password: _____   _____

Secret Key: ☐Start ☐End ☐Middle ☐Indicated Point ☐Split   _____
Key Used: ☐ 1 ☐ 2 ☐ 3 ☐ 4 ☐ 5 ☐ 6 ☐ 7

Account: _____   Additional Notes:

Username: _____   _____

Password: _____   _____

Secret Key: ☐Start ☐End ☐Middle ☐Indicated Point ☐Split   _____
Key Used: ☐ 1 ☐ 2 ☐ 3 ☐ 4 ☐ 5 ☐ 6 ☐ 7

Home Security Notes

Would you drive a car if you knew it had no brakes? Hopefully not.

It is surprising that most of us frequently choose to use technologies when we have no idea about the controls that are in place.

Although cybersecurity can seem like a really complicated subject to navigate, the basics are surprisingly simple. In the car scenario, you don't have to be a mechanic to know that driving a car with no brakes is a bad idea. So here are some simple steps that can help you to know how risky (or not) using any online device or application may be:

Firstly, any smart device (phone, tablet, laptop, ...) should always have up to date anti-malware in place. It may only catch 40% of the problems – but that is still 40% less risk.

Keep your device(s) up to date with the latest software operating system patches and anti-malware software updates. That will also significantly lower the chances of being compromised.

On any device where you hold information that you care about, never download any application from an untrusted source. You should also expect free applications to be looking to gather all kinds of information from the device you install it to. If you want to keep a device secure, be selective about what you 'trust' to install on it. Most corporate environments will usually have controls in place to stop you installing untrusted software.

When it comes to cybersecurity, people are still the most leveraged point of attack. Never click on a link from any email or IM conversation that you did not initiate. Criminals aim to pressure you in to thinking there is an urgency to click on a link – so equate any urgency to click on a link with a likelihood that it is a ploy to compromise your device.

You should also aim to maintain different (and hard to guess) passwords for different high-value online accounts. One of the first things that cyber criminals do if they manage to hack or intercept account information is to try that combination on Paypal, Amazon and other leading providers where they may be able to extract goods or money.

These days, it is not possible to be digitally bullet proof. Remember to back up your data and have a plan for how to recover your digital life. Any organization (and individual) should aim to be able to restore their devices (or configure new ones) with the minimum of pain and inconvenience when things go wrong.

Finally, if you do have to surf and visit websites of unknown provenance, try and do it from a device that holds no information of value – and make sure you do not swap files and media between that device and your clean environment.

Taken together, these simple steps can reduce your exposure to cyber attacks by over 80% - and mean that you can recover more easily if it does happen.

An interesting thing about the brakes on a car is that they are not really there to slow you down, they are actually a mechanism to allow you to drive faster. The same thing applies to these simple cybersecurity steps. Having the right cybersecurity controls in place lowers your risk and allows you to do more online.

A further and fuller publication on home and small business security can be purchased from www.cybersimplicity.com..